STUDENT
DPG # ATLAS of
WORLD POLITICS

D1495437

STUDENT ATLAS of WORLD POLITICS

DPG

John L. Allen
University of Connecticut

The Dushkin Publishing Group, Inc.

Printed in the United States of America

Library of Congress Catalog Card Number 93-073029

International Standard Book Number (ISBN) 1-56134-229-7

The Dushkin Publishing Group, Inc., Sluice Dock, Guilford, Connecticut 06437

A Note to the Student

International politics is a drama played out on a world stage. The maps in this atlas serve as the stage settings for the various scenes in this drama; the tables or data sets are the building materials from which the settings are created. Just as the stage setting helps bring to life and give meaning to the actions and words of a play, so can these maps and tables enhance your understanding of the vast and complex drama of global politics. Use this atlas in conjunction with your text on international politics or international affairs. It will help you become more knowledgeable of this international stage as well as the actors.

The maps and data sets in the *DGP Student Atlas of World Politics* are designed to introduce you to the importance of the connections between geography and world politics. The maps are not perfect representations of reality—no maps ever are—but they do represent "models" or approximations of the real world that should aid in your understanding of the world drama. At the very outset of your study of this atlas, you should be aware of some limitations of the maps and data tables. Because of the short time that has lapsed since the events surrounding the breakup of the Soviet Union and the disappearance of the Iron Curtain, there are simply no reliable economic, population, or other data for the many newly independent countries that have joined the world community since 1991. Hence, we have data on per capita income for the old USSR but we do not have separate data on per capita income for the 15 independent countries that were once part of the Soviet Union. Our decision has been to use the best data we can find in constructing our maps. In many instances this means "averaging" data so that, for example, the map of per capita income will show all former republics of the Soviet Union with the same per capita income figures. In subsequent editions of this atlas, we expect to have the same kind of reliable data on Byelorus, Ukraine, and the Czech Republic that we now have for the USSR and for Czechoslovakia. In the meantime, as events continue to restructure our world, it's an exciting time to be a student of international events!

You will find your study of this atlas more productive in relation to your study of international politics if you study the maps on the following pages in the context of five distinct themes:

1. *Location: Where Is It?* This theme offers a starting point from which you discover the precise location of places in both absolute terms (the latitude and longitude of a place) and in relative terms (the location of a place in relation to the location of other places). When you think of location, you should automatically think of both forms. Knowing something about absolute location will help you to understand a variety of features of physical geography, since such key elements are so closely related to their position on the Earth. But it is equally important to think of location in relative terms. Where places are located in relation to other places is often more important as a determinant of social, economic, and cultural characteristics than the factors of physical geography.

2. *Place: What Is It Like?* This theme investigates the political, economic, cultural, environmental, and other characteristics that give a place its identity. You should seek to understand the similarities and differences of places by exploring their basic characteristics. Why are some places with similar environmental characteristics so very different in economic, cultural, social, and political ways? Why are other places with such different environmental

characteristics so seemingly alike in terms of their institutions, their economies, and their cultures?

3. *Human/Environment Interactions: How Is the Landscape Shaped?* This theme illustrates the ways in which people respond to and modify their environments. On the world stage, humans are not the only part of the action. The environment also plays a role in the drama of international politics. But the characteristics of the environment do not exert a controlling influence over human activities; they only provide a set of alternatives from which different cultures, in different times, make their choices. Observe the relationship between the basic elements of physical geography such as climate and terrain and the host of ways in which humans have used the land surfaces of the world.

4. *Movement: How Do People Stay in Touch?* This theme examines the transportation and communication systems that link people and places. Movement or "spatial interaction" is the chief mechanism for the spread of ideas and innovations from one place to another. It is spatial interaction that validates the old cliché, "the world is getting smaller." We find McDonald's restaurants in Tokyo and Honda automobiles in New York City because of spatial interaction. Advanced transportation and communication systems have transformed the world into which your parents were born. And the world your children will be born into will be very different from your world. None of this would happen without the force of movement or spatial interaction.

5. *Regions: Worlds Within a World.* This theme, perhaps the most important for this atlas, helps to organize knowledge about the land and its people. The world consists of a mosaic of "regions" or areas that are somehow different and distinctive from other areas. The region of Anglo-America (the United States and Canada) is, for example, different enough from the region of Western Europe that geographers clearly identify them as two unique and separate areas. Yet despite their differences, Anglo-Americans and Europeans share a number of similarities: common cultural backgrounds, comparable economic patterns, shared religious traditions, and even some shared physical environmental characteristics. Conversely, although the regions of Anglo-America and Eastern Asia are also easily distinguished as distinctive units of the Earth's surface, those who live there have fewer similarities and more differences between them than is the case with Anglo-America and Western Europe: different cultural traditions, different institutions, different linguistic and religious patterns, and dissimilar natural environments. An understanding of both the differences and similarities between regions like Anglo-America and Western Europe on the one hand, or Anglo-America and Eastern Asia on the other, will help you to understand much that has happened in the human past or that is currently transpiring in the world around you. At the very least, an understanding of regional similarities and differences will help you to interpret what you read on the front page of your daily newspaper or view on the evening news report on your television set.

Not all of these themes will be immediately apparent on each of the 40 maps and 13 tables in this atlas. But if you study the contents of the *DPG Student Atlas of World Politics* along with the reading of your text and think about the five themes, the maps and your text will complement one another and improve your understanding of global politics. As Shakespeare said, "All the world's a stage." Your challenge is now to understand both the stage and the drama being played on it.

John L. Allen

Table of Contents

Part V. Food and Agriculture   55

Part VI. Energy and Materials   63

Part VII. Military   75

Part VIII. Environmental Conditions   83

Part I

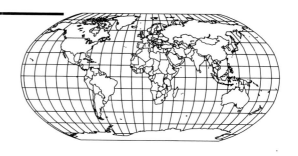

The Contemporary World

Map 1 Current World Political Boundaries

The international system includes states (countries) as the most important component.
The boundaries of countries are the most important source of political division in the
world, and for most people nationalism is the strongest source of political identification.

Scale: 1 to 125,000,000

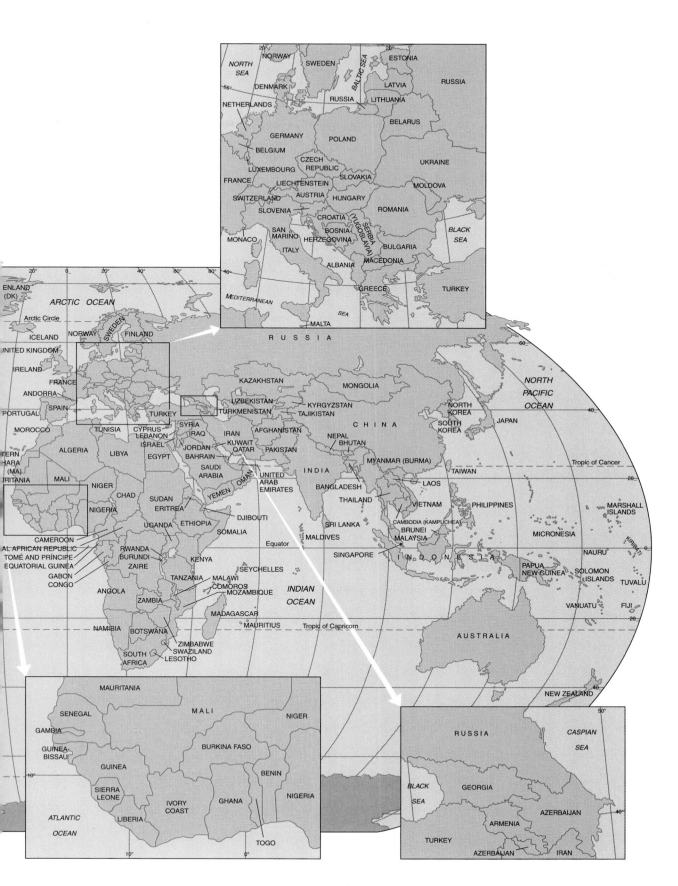

Map 2 World Climate Regions

Climates of the World

Tropical Moist Climates
- Rainforest
- Monsoon
- Savanna

Dry Climates
- Warm Desert
- Warm Steppe
- Cool Desert
- Cool Steppe

Mid-Latitude Climates
- Summer Dry or Mediterranean
- Moist Subtropical
- Marine West Coast
- Cool Forest
- Subarctic

Polar Climates
- Tundra
- Ice Cap

Azonal Climates
- Undifferentiated Highlands

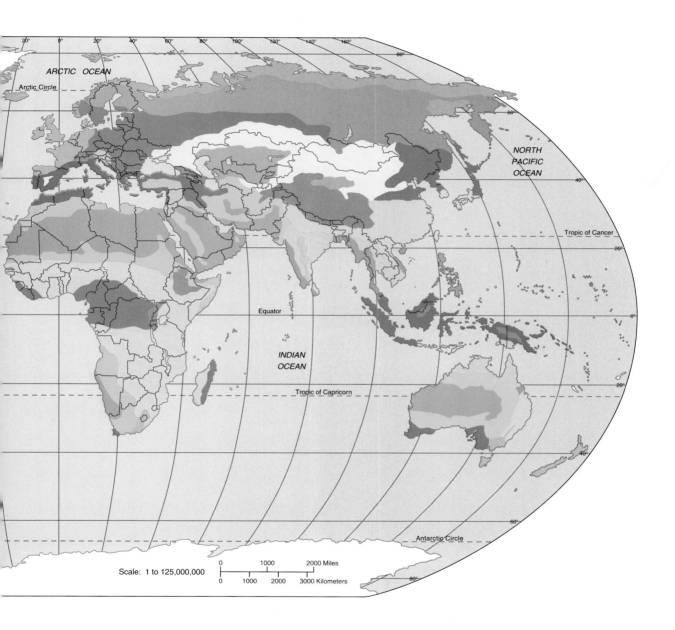

Of the world's many physical geographic features, climate (the long-term average of such weather conditions as temperature and precipitation) is the most important. It is climate that conditions the types of natural vegetation patterns and the types of soil that will exist in an area. It is also climate that determines the availability of our most precious resource: water. From an economic standpoint, the world's most important activity is agriculture; no other element of physical geography is more important for agriculture than climate.

Map 3 World Topography

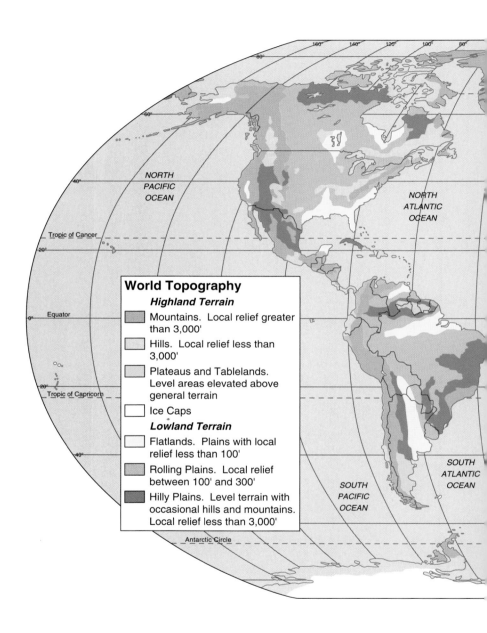

World Topography

Highland Terrain

Mountains. Local relief greater than 3,000'

Hills. Local relief less than 3,000'

Plateaus and Tablelands. Level areas elevated above general terrain

Ice Caps

Lowland Terrain

Flatlands. Plains with local relief less than 100'

Rolling Plains. Local relief between 100' and 300'

Hilly Plains. Level terrain with occasional hills and mountains. Local relief less than 3,000'

Second only to climate as a conditioner of human activity—particularly in agriculture and also in the location of cities and industry—is topography, or terrain. It is what we often call "landforms." A comparison of this map with the map of land use (Map 4) will show that most of the world's productive agricultural zones are located in the lowland regions. Where large regions of agricultural productivity are found, we also tend to find urban concentrations and, with cities, we find industry. There is also a good spatial correlation between the map of landforms and the map showing the distribution and density of the human population (Map 5). Normally, the world's landforms shown on

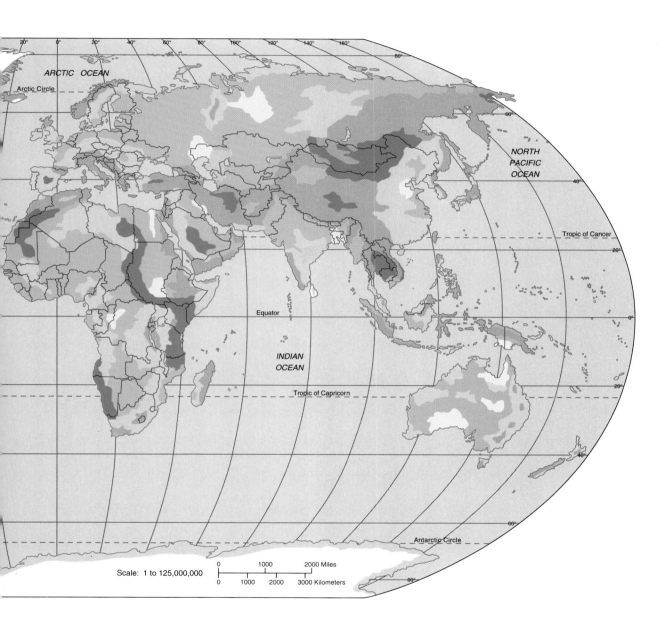

Scale: 1 to 125,000,000

| 0 | 1000 | | 2000 Miles |
| 0 | 1000 | 2000 | 3000 Kilometers |

this map are the result of extremely gradual primary geologic activity, such as the long-term movement of crustal plates (sometimes called continental drift). This activity occurs over hundreds of millions of years. Also important are the more rapid (but still slow by human standards) geomorphological or erosional activity of water, wind, glacial ice, and waves, tides, and currents. Some landforms may be produced by abrupt or cataclysmic events, such as a major volcanic eruption or a meteor strike, but these events are relatively rare and their effects are usually too minor to show up on a map of this scale.

Map 4 Land Use Patterns of the World

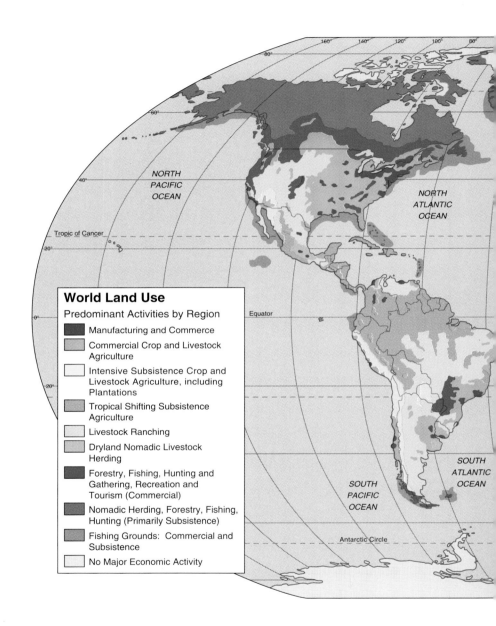

World Land Use

Predominant Activities by Region

- Manufacturing and Commerce
- Commercial Crop and Livestock Agriculture
- Intensive Subsistence Crop and Livestock Agriculture, including Plantations
- Tropical Shifting Subsistence Agriculture
- Livestock Ranching
- Dryland Nomadic Livestock Herding
- Forestry, Fishing, Hunting and Gathering, Recreation and Tourism (Commercial)
- Nomadic Herding, Forestry, Fishing, Hunting (Primarily Subsistence)
- Fishing Grounds: Commercial and Subsistence
- No Major Economic Activity

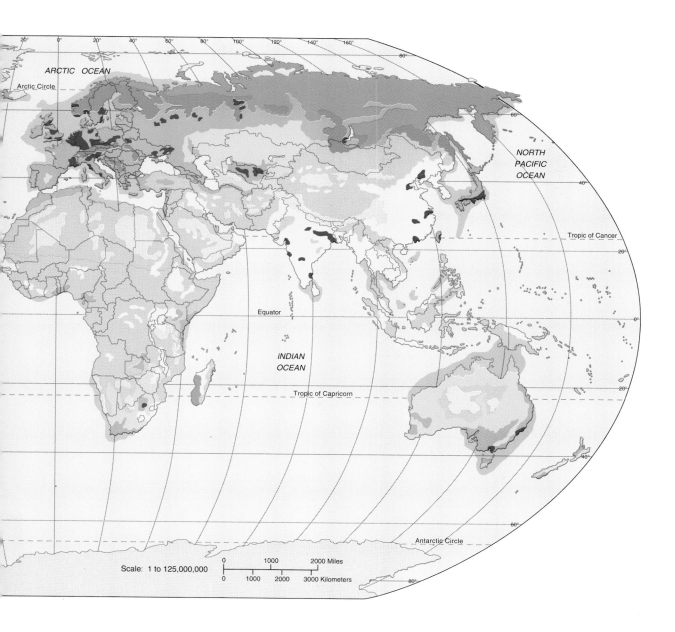

Many of the major land use patterns of the world (such as urbanization, industry, and transportation) are relatively small in area and are not easily seen on maps, but the most important uses people make of the Earth's surface have more far-reaching effects. This map illustrates, in particular, the variations in primary land uses (such as agriculture) for the entire world. Note particularly the differences between land use patterns in the more developed countries of the temperate zones and the lesser developed countries of the tropics.

Map 5 World Population Density

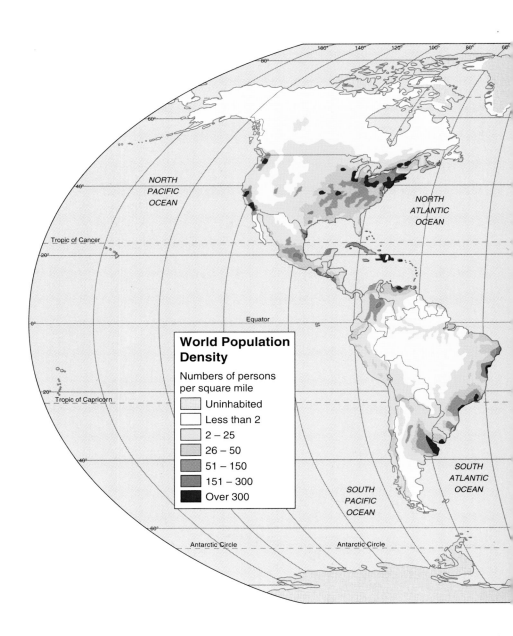

World Population Density

Numbers of persons per square mile

- Uninhabited
- Less than 2
- 2 – 25
- 26 – 50
- 51 – 150
- 151 – 300
- Over 300

No feature of human activity is more reflective of environmental conditions than where people live. In the areas of densest populations, combinations of natural and human factors have combined to allow maximum food production, maximum urbanization, and great concentrations of economic activities. Three main centers of human population appear on the map—East Asia, South Asia, and Europe—with a fourth lesser concentration in eastern North America (the "Megalopolis" region of the United States and Canada). One of these great population clusters—South Asia—is still growing rapidly and can be expected to become even more densely populated by the beginning of the twenty-first century. The other concentrations are likely to remain about as

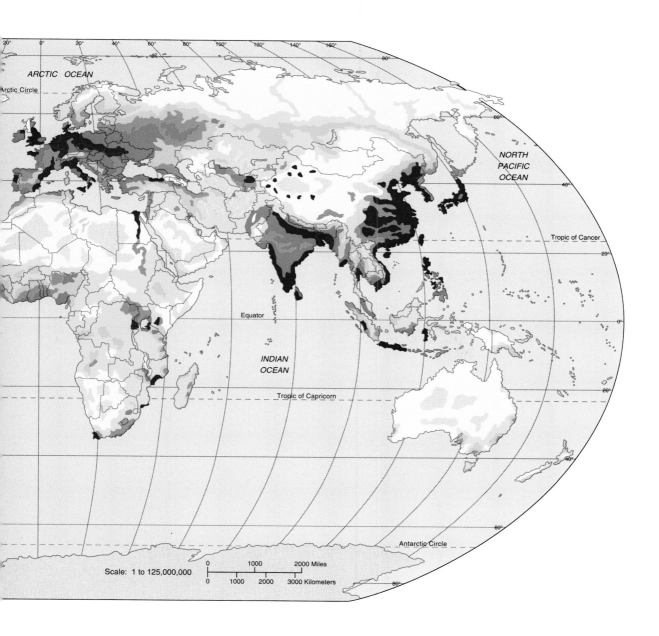

they now appear. In Europe and North America, this is the result of economic development that has caused population growth to level off during the last century. In East Asia, population has also begun to grow more slowly. In the case of Japan and the Koreas, this is the consequence of economic development; in the case of China, it is the consequence of government intervention in the form of strict family planning. The areas of future high density (in addition to those already existing) are likely to be in Latin America and Africa, where population growth rates are well above the world average.

Table A

World Countries: Area, Population, and Population Density, 1992

COUNTRY	AREA (mi^2)	POPULATION (1992 est.)	DENSITY (pop/mi^2)
Afghanistan	251,826	16,880,000	67
Albania	11,100	3,352,000	302
Algeria	919,595	26,360,000	29
Angola	481,354	10,425,000	22
Antigua and Barbuda	171	64,000	374
Argentina	1,073,400	32,860,000	31
Armenia	11,506	3,360,000	292
Australia	2,966,155	17,420,000	6
Austria	32,377	7,681,000	237
Azerbaijan	33,436	7,170,000	214
Bahamas	5,382	260,000	48
Bahrain	267	546,000	2,045
Bangladesh	55,598	118,000,000	2,122
Barbados	166	257,000	1,548
Belarus	80,155	10,390,000	130
Belgium	11,783	9,932,000	843
Belize	8,866	232,000	26
Benin	43,475	4,914,000	113
Bhutan	17,954	1,614,000	90
Bolivia	424,165	7,243,000	17
Bosnia-Herzegovina	19,741	4,519,000	229
Botswana	224,711	1,345,000	6
Brazil	3,286,488	156,750,000	48
Brunei	2,226	411,000	185
Bulgaria	42,823	8,902,000	208
Burkina Faso	105,869	9,510,000	90
Burundi	10,745	5,924,000	551
Cambodia	69,898	8,543,000	122
Cameroon	183,569	11,550,000	63
Canada	3,849,674	26,985,000	7
Cape Verde	1,557	393,000	252
Central African Republic	240,535	2,990,000	12
Chad	495,755	5,178,000	10
Chile	292,135	13,395,000	46
China	3,689,631	1,181,580,000	320
Colombia	440,831	33,170,000	75
Comoros	863	484,000	561
Congo	132,047	2,344,000	18
Costa Rica	19,730	3,151,000	160
Croatia	21,829	4,800,000	220
Cuba	42,804	10,785,000	252
Cyprus	2,276	713,000	313
Czechoslovakia[1]	49,382	15,755,000	319
Denmark	16,638	5,154,000	310
Djibouti	8,958	351,000	39
Dominica	305	87,000	285
Dominican Republic	18,704	8,124,000	434
Ecuador	109,484	10,880,000	99
Egypt	386,662	55,105,000	143
El Salvador	8,124	5,473,000	674
Equatorial Guinea	10,831	384,000	35
Estonia	17,413	1,606,000	92
Ethiopia	483,123	54,040,000	112
Fiji	7,078	747,000	106
Finland	130,559	5,001,000	38
France	211,208	57,010,000	270
Gabon	103,347	1,088,000	11
Gambia	4,127	889,000	215
Georgia	26,911	5,550,000	206

(continued on next page)

COUNTRY	AREA (mi^2)	POPULATION (1992 est.)	DENSITY (pop/mi^2)
Germany	137,882	79,710,000	578
Ghana	92,098	15,865,000	172
Greece	50,962	10,285,000	202
Grenada	133	98,000	737
Guatemala	42,042	9,386,000	223
Guinea	94,926	7,553,000	80
Guinea-Bissau	13,948	1,036,000	74
Guyana	83,000	748,000	9
Haiti	10,714	6,361,000	594
Honduras	43,277	5,342,000	123
Hungary	35,920	10,555,000	294
Iceland	36,769	261,000	6.6
India	1,237,062	874,150,000	707
Indonesia	752,410	195,300,000	260
Iran	632,457	60,000,000	95
Iraq	169,235	19,915,000	118
Ireland	27,137	3,484,000	128
Israel	8,019	4,393,000	548
Italy	116,234	57,830,000	497
Ivory Coast	124,518	13,240,000	106
Jamaica	4,244	2,501,000	589
Japan	145,870	124,270,000	852
Jordan	35,135	3,485,000	99
Kazakhstan	1,049,156	16,880,000	16
Kenya	224,961	25,695,000	114
Korea, North	46,540	22,250,000	478
Korea, South	38,230	43,305,000	1,133
Kuwait	6,880	2,244,000	326
Kyrgyzstan	76,641	4,385,000	57
Laos	91,429	4,158,000	45
Latvia	24,595	2,737,000	111
Lebanon	4,015	3,049,000	849
Lesotho	11,720	1,824,000	156
Liberia	38,250	2,776,000	73
Libya	679,362	4,416,000	6.5
Liechtenstein	62	28,000	452
Lithuania	25,174	3,767,000	150
Luxembourg	998	390,000	391
Macedonia	9928	2,120,000	214
Madagascar	226,658	12,380,000	55
Malawi	45,747	9,523,000	208
Malaysia	129,251	18,200,000	141
Maldives	115	230,000	2,000
Mali	478,767	8,438,000	18
Malta	122	357,000	2,926
Mauritania	395,956	2,028,000	5.1
Mauritius	788	1,085,000	1,377
Mexico	756,066	91,000,000	120
Micronesia	271	109,000	402
Moldova	13,012	4,440,000	341
Monaco	.6	29,712	4,952
Mongolia	604,829	2,278,000	3.8
Morocco	172,414	26,470,000	154
Mozambique	308,642	15,460,000	50
Myanmar	261,228	42,615,000	163
Namibia	317,818	1,548,000	4.9
Nauru	8	9,333	1,166
Nepal	56,827	19,845,000	349
Netherlands	16,133	15,065,000	934
New Zealand	103,519	3,463,000	33
Nicaragua	50,054	3,805,000	76
Niger	489,191	8,113,000	17
Nigeria	356,669	124,300,000	349
Norway	149,412	4,286,000	29
Oman	82,030	1,562,000	19

(continued on next page)

COUNTRY	AREA (mi^2)	POPULATION (1992 est.)	DENSITY (pop/mi^2)
Pakistan	339,732	119,000,000	350
Panama	29,157	2,503,000	86
Papua New Guinea	178,704	3,960,000	22
Paraguay	157,048	4,871,000	31
Peru	496,225	22,585,000	46
Philippines	115,831	62,380,000	539
Poland	120,728	37,840,000	313
Portugal	35,516	10,410,000	293
Qatar	4,416	532,000	120
Romania	91,699	23,465,000	256
Russia	6,592,849	150,505,000	23
Rwanda	10,169	8,053,000	792
St. Kitts and Nevis	104	42,000	404
St. Lucia	238	155,000	651
St. Vincent and the Grenadines	150	115,000	767
Saõ Tomé and Príncipe	372	130,000	349
Saudi Arabia	830,000	16,690,000	20
Senegal	75,951	7,569,000	100
Serbia (Yugoslavia)	34,116	9,975,000	292
Seychelles	175	69,000	394
Sierra Leone	27,925	4,330,000	155
Singapore	246	3,062,000	12,447
Slovenia	7,819	1,989.000	254
Solomon Islands	10,954	353,000	32
Somalia	246,201	6,823,000	28
South Africa	433,680	36,765,000	85
Spain	194,885	39,465,000	203
Sri Lanka	24,962	17,530,000	702
Sudan	967,500	27,630,000	29
Suriname	63,251	405,000	6.4
Swaziland	6,704	875,000	131
Sweden	173,732	8,581,000	49
Switzerland	15,943	6,804,000	427
Syria	71,498	13,210,000	185
Taiwan	13,900	20,785,000	1,495
Tajikistan	55,251	5,210,000	94
Tanzania	364,900	27,325,000	75
Thailand	198,115	57,200,000	289
Togo	21,925	3,880,000	177
Tonga	270	102,000	377
Trinidad and Tobago	1,980	1,293,000	653
Tunisia	63,170	8,367,000	132
Turkey	300,948	58,850,000	196
Turkmenistan	188,456	3,615,000	19
Uganda	93,104	18,485,000	199
Ukraine	233,090	52,800,000	227
United Arab Emirates	32,278	2,459,000	76
United Kingdom	94,248	57,630,000	611
United States	3,787,425	253,510,000	67
Uruguay	68,500	3,130,000	46
Uzbekistan	172,742	20,325,000	118
Vanuatu	4,707	153,000	33
Venezuela	352,145	20,430,000	58
Vietnam	128,066	68,310,000	533
Yemen	205,356	11,825,000	58
Zaire	905,446	38,475,000	42
Zambia	290,586	8,201,000	28
Zimbabwe	150,873	9,748,000	65

[1]On January 1, 1993, Czechoslovakia was separated by peaceful agreement into two independent countries, the Czech Republic and the Slovak Republic. At the time of this printing, information was not yet available for these two separate countries.

Sources: The World Almanac and Book of Facts 1993 (Scripps Howard, New York); *Goode's World Atlas*, 18th edition (Rand McNally, Chicago).

Part II

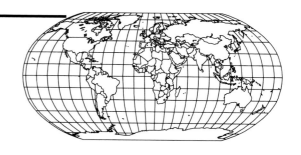

Historical Developments in the Modern Era

Map 6 National Dates of Independence

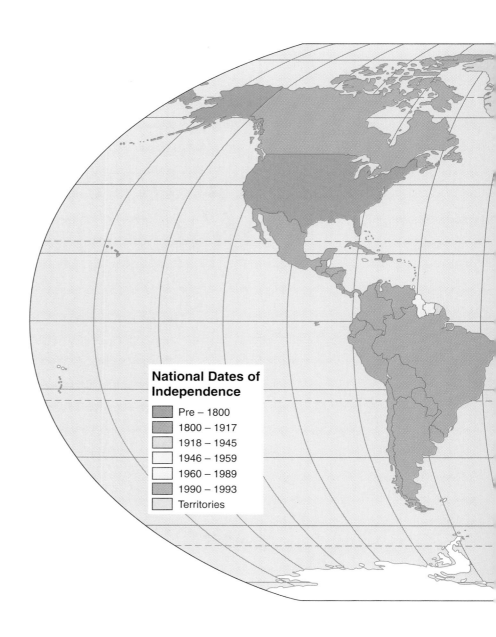

National Dates of Independence

- Pre – 1800
- 1800 – 1917
- 1918 – 1945
- 1946 – 1959
- 1960 – 1989
- 1990 – 1993
- Territories

Most countries of the modern world, including such major states as Germany and Italy, have become independent since the beginning of the last century. Of the world's current countries, only 23 were independent in 1800. (More than half of the 23 were in Europe; the others were Afghanistan, China, Ethiopia, Japan, Iran, Nepal, Oman, Russia, Thailand, Turkey, and the United States. Following 1800 there have been four great periods of national independence. During the first of these (1800–1917), most of the independent mainland countries of the Americas achieved independence. During the second period (1918–1945), the countries of Eastern Europe emerged as inde-

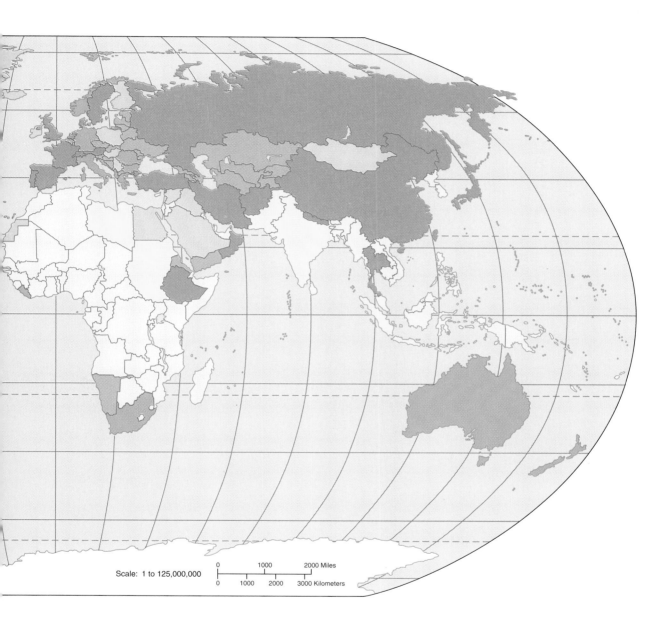

Scale: 1 to 125,000,000

| 0 | | 1000 | | 2000 Miles |
| 0 | 1000 | 2000 | 3000 Kilometers | |

pendent entities. The third period (1946–1959) followed World War II, when independence for African and Asian nations that had been under control of colonial powers
first began to occur. During the fourth period (1960–present), independence came to
the remainder of the colonial African and Asian nations, as well as to former colonies
in the Caribbean and the South Pacific. More than half of the world's independent
countries have come into being as independent political entities in the last three decades. During the past few years alone, for example, the breakup of Czechoslovakia,
the Soviet Union, and Yugoslavia created 22 countries where only 3 had existed before.

Map 7 Post–World War II Europe

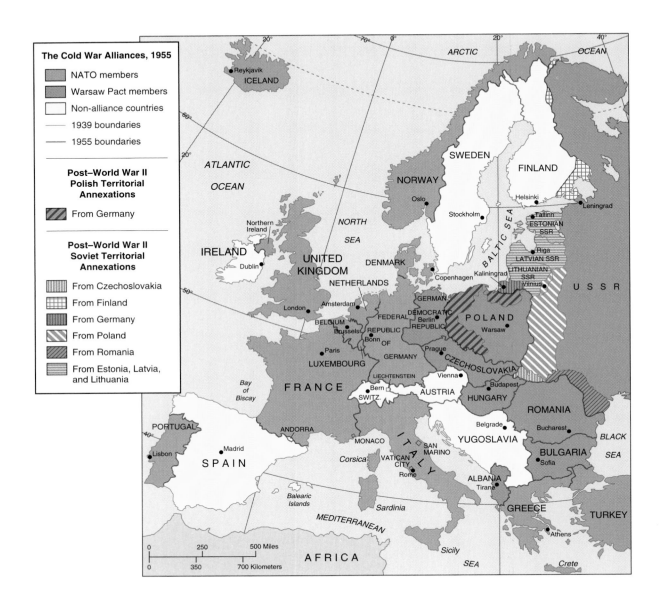

The Cold War Alliances, 1955

- NATO members
- Warsaw Pact members
- Non-alliance countries
- 1939 boundaries
- 1955 boundaries

Post–World War II Polish Territorial Annexations

- From Germany

Post–World War II Soviet Territorial Annexations

- From Czechoslovakia
- From Finland
- From Germany
- From Poland
- From Romania
- From Estonia, Latvia, and Lithuania

The East-West struggle that dominated world politics for about 40 years was epitomized by the opposing cold war alliances of NATO, formed in 1949, and the Warsaw Pact, founded in 1955. With the end of the cold war, many of the territorial adjustments made between 1939 and 1946 were unfrozen. Some people believe that Germany may one day press Poland for the return of lands given to Poland after World War II.

Map 8 Post–Cold War Europe

Eurasian countries

ICELAND

IRELAND
Dublin
Northern Ireland

UNITED KINGDOM
London

NORWAY
Oslo

SWEDEN
Stockholm

FINLAND
Helsinki

DENMARK
Copenhagen

NETHERLANDS
Amsterdam

BELGIUM
Brussels

LUXEMBOURG

FRANCE
Paris

ANDORRA

SPAIN
Madrid

PORTUGAL
Lisbon
Gibraltar (UK)

GERMANY
Berlin
Bonn

POLAND
Warsaw

CZECH REPUBLIC
Prague

SLOVAKIA
Bratislava

AUSTRIA
Vienna

SWITZ.
Bern

LIECHTENSTEIN

HUNGARY
Budapest

SLOVENIA
Ljubljana

CROATIA
Zagreb

BOSNIA-HERZEGOVINA
Sarajevo

YUGOSLAVIA
Belgrade

ITALY
Rome
SAN MARINO
VATICAN CITY
MONACO

ALBANIA
Tirane

MACEDONIA
Skopje

BULGARIA
Sofia

ROMANIA
Bucharest

MOLDOVA
Kishinev

UKRAINE
Kiev

BELARUS
Minsk

LITHUANIA
Vilnius

RUSSIA
Kaliningrad

LATVIA
Riga

ESTONIA
Tallinn

RUSSIA
Moscow

KAZAKHSTAN

URALS

GEORGIA
Tbilisi

ARMENIA
Yerevan

AZERBAIJAN
Baku

IRAN

IRAQ

SYRIA

LEBANON

CYPRUS

TURKEY
Ankara

GREECE
Athens

Crete

MALTA

Sicily

Sardinia

Corsica

Balearic Islands

AFRICA

MEDITERRANEAN SEA

BLACK SEA

CASPIAN SEA

BALTIC SEA

NORTH SEA

ATLANTIC OCEAN

Bay of Biscay

20°
60°
0°
20°

500 Miles
700 Kilometers
0 250 350
0

The map of contemporary Europe encapsulates the crosscutting forces that are affecting the international system. Growing economic unity and political cooperation characterize the countries of Western Europe. Eastern Europe, by contrast, has become fragmented; about half the region's countries were not independent when the 1990s began. Perhaps most important, the political geographic definition of Europe itself has changed with the addition of such former Soviet republics as Estonia, Latvia, Lithuania, Belarus, Ukraine, and Moldova to the list of states that are now considered "European."

Map ⏹9 The Breakup of the Soviet Union

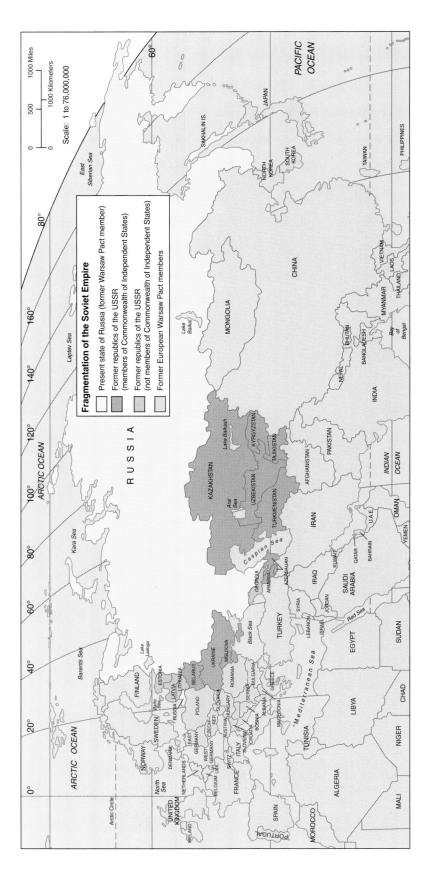

Seldom in world history has there been such a sweeping change of the political map in the absence of major military conflict as there has been since 1990. The former Soviet Union has fragmented into 15 independent states, only 11 of which are loosely bound together in the new Commonwealth of Independent States. East Germany has been reunited with West Germany. Czechoslovakia and Yugoslavia have both fragmented, the former into two independent states, the latter into five.

Map 10 The Middle East: Territorial Changes, 1918–Present

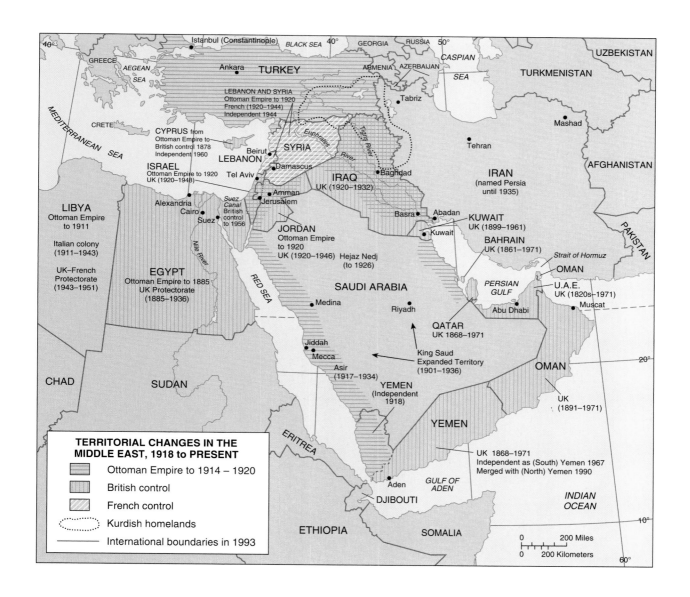

TERRITORIAL CHANGES IN THE MIDDLE EAST, 1918 to PRESENT

- Ottoman Empire to 1914 – 1920
- British control
- French control
- Kurdish homelands
- International boundaries in 1993

The Middle East, encompassing the northeastern part of Africa and southwestern Asia, has experienced a turbulent history. In the last century alone, many of the region's countries have gone from being ruled by the Turkish Ottoman Empire, to being dependencies of Great Britain or France, to being independent. Having experienced the Crusades and colonial domination by European powers, the region's predominantly Islamic countries are now resentful of interference in the region's affairs by countries with a European and/or Christian heritage.

Map 11 Africa: Colonialism to Independence, 1910–1993

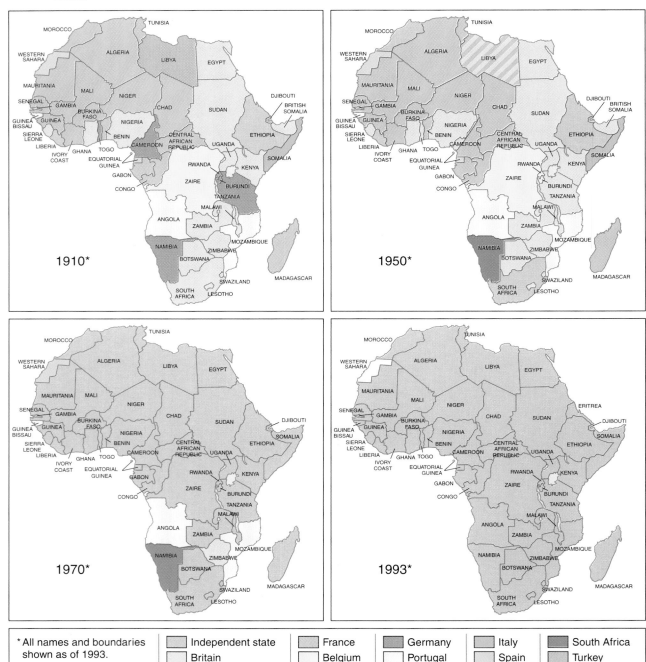

1910*

1950*

1970*

1993*

* All names and boundaries shown as of 1993.

Independent state	France
Britain	Belgium

Germany	Italy
Portugal	Spain

South Africa
Turkey

In few parts of the world has the transition from colonialism to independence been as abrupt as it has been on the African continent. Unlike Middle and South America, most of whose states achieved independence from their colonial masters in the early nineteenth century, the independence of African states is primarily a twentieth-century affair, with much of the independence taking place after World War II. In part because of their recent status as independent countries with borders that are legacies of their former colonial status, many African states are beset by internal problems related to tribal and ethnic conflicts. (Western Sahara is not yet independent.)

Map 12 Asia: Colonialism to Independence, 1930–1993

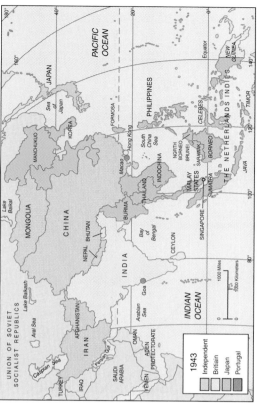

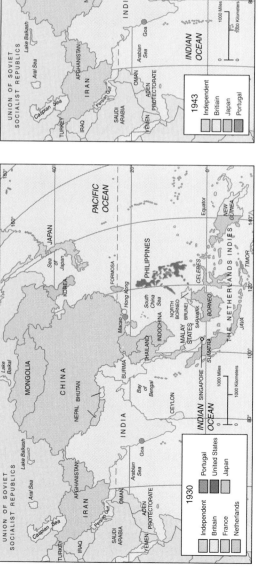

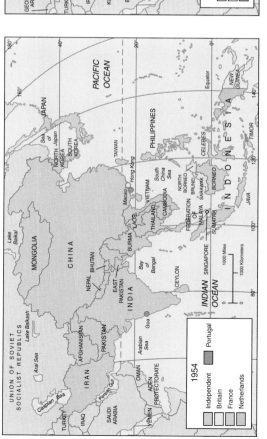

Asian countries, like those in Africa, have recently emerged from a colonial past. With the exception of China, Japan, and Thailand, virtually all Asian nations were until recently under the colonial control of Great Britain, France, the Netherlands, or the United States. Japan itself was, for a short period of time between 1930 and 1945, a colonial power with considerable territories on the Asian mainland. The unraveling of colonial control in Asia, particularly in South and Southeast Asia, has precipitated internal conflicts in the newly independent states that are still a major part of the political geography of the region.

Table B

World Countries: Form of Government, Capital City, and Major Languages

COUNTRY	FORM OF GOVERNMENT	CAPITAL	MAJOR LANGUAGES
Afghanistan	Republic	Kabul	Dari, Pashton, Uzbek, Turkmen
Albania	Socialist republic	Tiranë	Albanian, Greek
Algeria	Socialist republic	Algiers	Arabic, Berber dialects, French
Angola	Socialist republic	Luanda	Portugese, indigenous
Antigua and Barbuda	Constitutional monarchy	St. John's	English
Argentina	Republic	Buenos Aires	Spanish, English, Italian, German
Armenia	Republic	Yerevan	Armenian, Azerbaijani, Russian
Australia	Federal parliamentary	Canberra	English, indigenous
Austria	Federal republic	Vienna	German
Azerbaijan	Republic	Baku	Azerbaijani, Russian, Armenian
Bahamas	Independent commonwealth	Nassau	English
Bahrain	Monarchy	Al-Manamah	Arabic, English, Farsi, Urdu
Bangladesh	Islamic republic	Dhaka	Bangla, English
Barbados	Parliamentary state	Bridgetown	English
Belarus	Republic	Minsk	Byelorussian, Russian
Belgium	Constititional monarchy	Brussels	Dutch (Flemish), French, German
Belize	Parliamentary state	Belmopan	English, Spanish, Garifuna, Mayan
Benin	Republic	Porto-Novo	French, Fon, Adja, indigenous
Bhutan	Monarchy	Thimphu	Dzongha, Tibetan, Nepalese
Bolivia	Republic	La Paz	Spanish, Quechua, Aymara
Bosnia-Herzegovina	Republic	Sarajevo	Serb, Croat, Albanian
Botswana	Republic	Gaborone	English, Tswania
Brazil	Federal republic	Brasília	Portugese, Spanish, English, French
Brunei	Monarchy	Bandar Seri Begawan	Malay, English, Chinese
Bulgaria	Republic	Sofia	Bulgarian
Burkina Faso	Provisional military	Ouagadougou	French, indigenous
Burundi	Provisional military	Bujumbura	French, Kirundi, Swahili
Cambodia	Socialist republic	Phnom Penh	Khmer, French
Cameroon	Republic	Yaoundé	English, French, indigenous
Canada	Federal parliamentary	Ottawa	English, French
Cape Verde	Republic	Praia	Portugese, Crioulu
Central African Republic	Republic	Bangui	French, Sango, Arabic, indigenous
Chad	Republic	N'Djamena	Arabic, French, indigenous
Chile	Republic	Santiago	Spanish
China	Socialist republic	Beijing	Chinese dialects
Colombia	Republic	Bogotá	Spanish
Comoros	Federal Islamic republic	Moroni	Arabic, French, Shaafi Islam
Congo	Socialist republic	Brazzaville	French, indigenous
Costa Rica	Republic	San José	Spanish
Croatia	Republic	Zagreb	Croat, Serb
Cuba	Socialist republic	Havana	Spanish
Cyprus	Republic	Nicosia	Greek, Turkish, English
Czechoslovakia[1]	Federal republic	Prague	Czech, Slovak, Hungarian
Denmark	Constitutional monarchy	Copenhagen	Danish
Djibouti	Republic	Djibouti	French, Somali, Afar, Arabic
Dominica	Republic	Roseau	English, French
Dominican Republic	Republic	Santo Domingo	Spanish
Ecuador	Republic	Quito	Spanish, Quechua, indigenous
Egypt	Socialist republic	Cairo	Arabic
El Salvador	Republic	San Salvador	Spanish, Nahua
Equatorial Guinea	Republic	Malabo	Spanish, indigenous, English
Estonia	Republic	Tallinn	Estonian, Russian
Ethiopia	Socialist republic	Addis Ababa	Amharic, Tigrinya, Orominga, Arabic
Fiji	Republic	Suva	English, Fijian, Hindustani
Finland	Republic	Helsinki	Finnish, Swedish
France	Republic	Paris	French
Gabon	Republic	Libreville	French, Fang, indigenous
Gambia	Republic	Banjul	English, Malinke, Wolof, Fula

(continued on next page)

COUNTRY	FORM OF GOVERNMENT	CAPITAL	MAJOR LANGUAGES
Georgia	Republic	Tbilisi	Georgian, Russian, Armenian
Germany	Federal republic	Berlin and Bonn	German
Ghana	Provisional military	Accra	English, Akan, indigenous
Greece	Republic	Athens	Greek
Grenada	Parliamentary state	St. George's	English, French
Guatemala	Republic	Guatemala	Spanish, indigenous
Guinea	Provisional military	Conakry	French, indigenous
Guinea-Bissau	Republic	Bissau	Portugese, Crioulo, indigenous
Guyana	Republic	Georgetown	English, indigenous
Haiti	Republic	Port-au-Prince	Creole, French
Honduras	Republic	Tegucigalpa	Spanish, indigenous
Hungary	Republic	Budapest	Hungarian
Iceland	Republic	Reykjavík	Icelandic
India	Federal republic	New Delhi	English, Hindi, Telugu, Bengali
Indonesia	Republic	Jakarta	Indonesian, Javanese, Sundanese
Iran	Islamic republic	Tehran	Farsi, Turkish, Kurdish, Arabic, English
Iraq	Republic	Baghdad	Arabic, Kurdish, Assyrian, Armenian
Ireland	Republic	Dublin	English, Irish Gaelic
Israel	Republic	Jerusalem	Hebrew, Arabic, Yiddish
Ivory Coast	Republic	Abidjan	French, indigenous
Italy	Republic	Rome	Italian
Jamaica	Parliamentary state	Kingston	English, Creole
Japan	Constitutional monarchy	Tokyo	Japanese
Jordan	Constitutional monarchy	Amman	Arabic
Kazakhstan	Republic	Alma-Ata	Kazakh, Russian, German, Ukranian
Kenya	Republic	Nairobi	English, Swahili, indigenous
Korea, North	Socialist republic	P'yongyang	Korean
Korea, South	Republic	Seoul	Korean
Kuwait	Constitutional monarchy	Kuwait	Arabic, English
Kyrgyzstan	Republic	Bishkek	Kirghiz, Russian, Uzbek
Laos	Socialist republic	Vientiane	Lao, French, Thai, indigenous
Latvia	Republic	Riga	Latvian, Russian
Lebanon	Republic	Beirut	Arabic, French, Armenian, English
Lesotho	Constitutional monarchy	Maseru	English, Sesotho, Zulu, Xhosa
Liberia	Republic	Monrovia	English, indigenous
Libya	Socialist republic	Tripoli	Arabic
Liechtenstein	Constitutional monarchy	Vaduz	German
Lithuania	Republic	Vilnius	Lithuanian, Russian, Polish
Luxembourg	Constitutional monarchy	Luxembourg	French, Luxembourgish, German
Macedonia	Republic	Skopje	Macedonian, Albanian
Madagascar	Republic	Antananarivo	Malagasy, French
Malawi	Republic	Lilongwe	Chichewa, English, Tombuka
Malaysia	Federal constitutional monarchy	Kuala Lumpur	Malay, Chinese, English
Maldives	Republic	Male	Divehi
Mali	Republic	Bamako	French, Bambara, indigenous
Malta	Republic	Valletta	English, Maltese
Mauritania	Provisional military	Nouakchott	Arabic, French, indigenous
Mauritius	Parliamentary state	Port Louis	English, Creole, Bhojpun, Hindi
Mexico	Federal republic	Mexico City	Spanish, indigenous
Micronesia	Republic	Kolonia	English, Malay-Polynesian languages
Moldova	Republic	Kishinev	Moldavian, Russian, Ukrainian
Monaco	Constitutional monarchy	Monaco	French, Italian
Mongolia	Socialist republic	Ulan Bator	Khalkha Mongol, Kazakh, Russian
Morocco	Constitutional monarchy	Rabat	Arabic, Berber dialects, French
Mozambique	Republic	Maputo	Portuguese, indigenous
Myanmar	Provisional military	Yangon	Burmese, indigenous
Namibia	Republic	Windhoek	Afrikaans, English, German, indigenous
Nauru	Republic	Yaren	Nauruan, other indigenous
Nepal	Constitutional monarchy	Katmandu	Nepali, Maithali, Bhojpuri, indigenous
Netherlands	Constitutional monarchy	Amsterdam	Dutch
New Zealand	Parliamentary state	Wellington	English, Maori
Nicaragua	Republic	Managua	Spanish, English, indigenous
Niger	Provisional military	Niamey	French, Hausa, Djerma, indigenous
Nigeria	Provisional military	Lagos/Abuja	English, Hausa, Fulani, Yorbua, Ibo
Norway	Constitutional monarchy	Oslo	Norwegian, Lapp
Oman	Monarchy	Muscat	Arabic, English, Baluchi, Urdu

(continued on next page)

COUNTRY	FORM OF GOVERNMENT	CAPITAL	MAJOR LANGUAGES
Pakistan	Federal Islamic republic	Islamabad	English, Urdu, Punjabi, Pashto, Sindhi
Panama	Republic	Panama	Spanish, English, indigenous
Papua New Guinea	Parliamentary state	Port Moresby	English, Motu, Pidgin, indigenous
Paraguay	Republic	Asunción	Spanish, Guarani
Peru	Republic	Lima	Quechua, Spanish, Aymara
Philippines	Republic	Manila	English, Pilipino, Tagalog
Poland	Republic	Warsaw	Polish
Portugal	Republic	Lisbon	Portuguese
Qatar	Monarchy	Doha	Arabic, English
Romania	Republic	Bucharest	Romanian, Hungarian, German
Russia	Republic	Moscow	Russian, Tatar, Ukranian
Rwanda	Provisional military	Kigali	French, Kinyarwanda
St. Kitts and Nevis	Parliamentary state	Basseterre	English
St. Lucia	Parliamentary state	Castries	English, French
St. Vincent and the Grenadines	Parliamentary state	Kingstown	English, French
São Tomé and Príncipe	Republic	São Tomé	Portuguese, Fang
Saudi Arabia	Monarchy	Riyadh	Arabic
Senegal	Republic	Dakar	French, Wolof, indigenous
Serbia (Yugoslavia)	Republic	Belgrade	Serb, Albanian, Hungarian
Seychelles	Republic	Victoria	English, French, Creole
Sierra Leone	Republic	Freetown	English, Krio, indigenous
Singapore	Republic	Singapore	Mandarin Chinese, English, Malay
Slovenia	Republic	Ljubljana	Slovene
Solomon Islands	Parliamentary state	Honiara	English, Malay-Polynesian languages
Somalia	Provisional military	Mogadishu	Arabic, Somali, English, Italian
South Africa	Republic	Pretoria	Afrikaans, English, Zulu, Xhosa, other
Spain	Constitutional monarchy	Madrid	Spanish, Catalan, Galician. Basque
Sri Lanka	Socialist republic	Colombo	English, Sinhala, Tamil
Sudan	Islamic republic	Khartoum	Arabic, indigenous, English
Suriname	Republic	Paramaribo	Dutch, Sranan Tongo, English
Swaziland	Monarchy	Mbabane	English, Swahili
Sweden	Constitutional monarchy	Stockholm	Swedish
Switzerland	Federal republic	Bern	German, French, Italian, Romansch
Syria	Socialist republic	Damascus	Arabic, Kurdish, Armenian, Aramaic
Taiwan	Republic	Taipei	Chinese dialects
Tajikistan	Republic	Dushanbe	Tajik, Uzbek, Russian
Tanzania	Republic	Dar es Salaam	English, Swahili, indigenous
Thailand	Constitutional monarchy	Bangkok	Thai, indigenous
Togo	Republic	Lomé	French, indigenous
Tonga	Constitutional monarchy	Nuku'alofa	Tongan, English
Trinidad and Tobago	Republic	Port of Spain	English, Hindi, French, Spanish
Tunisia	Republic	Tunis	Arabic, French
Turkey	Republic	Ankara	Turkish, Kurdish, Arabic
Turkmenistan	Republic	Ashkhabad	Turkmen, Russian, Uzbek, Kazakh
Uganda	Republic	Kampala	English, Luganda, Swahili, indigenous
Ukraine	Republic	Kiev	Ukranian, Russian
United Arab Emirates	Federated monarchy	Abu Dhabi	Arabic, English, Farsi, Hindi, Urdu
United Kingdom	Constitutional monarchy	London	English, Welsh, Gaelic
United States	Federal republic	Washington	English, Spanish
Uruguay	Republic	Montevideo	Spanish
Uzbekistan	Republic	Tashkent	Uzbek, Russian, Kazakh, Tajik, Tatar
Vanuatu	Republic	Port-Vila	Bislama, French, English
Venezuela	Federal republic	Caracas	Spanish, indigenous
Vietnam	Socialist republic	Hanoi	Vietnamese, French, Chinese, English
Yemen	Republic	San'a	Arabic
Zaire	Republic	Kinshasa	French, Kikongo, Lingala, Swahili
Zambia	Republic	Lusaka	English, Tonga, Lozi, other indigenous
Zimbabwe	Republic	Harare	English, ChiShona, SiNdebele

[1]On January 1, 1993, Czechoslovakia was separated by peaceful agreement into two independent countries, the Czech Republic and the Slovak Republic. At the time of this printing, information was not yet available for these two separate countries.

Sources: The World Almanac and Book of Facts 1993 (Scripps Howard, New York); *Goode's World Atlas*, 18th edition (Rand McNally, Chicago); U.S. Central Intelligence Agency.

Part III

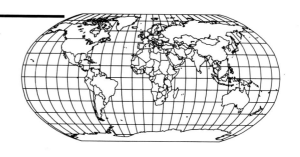

The Global Economy

Map 13 Total GNP and GNP Per Capita

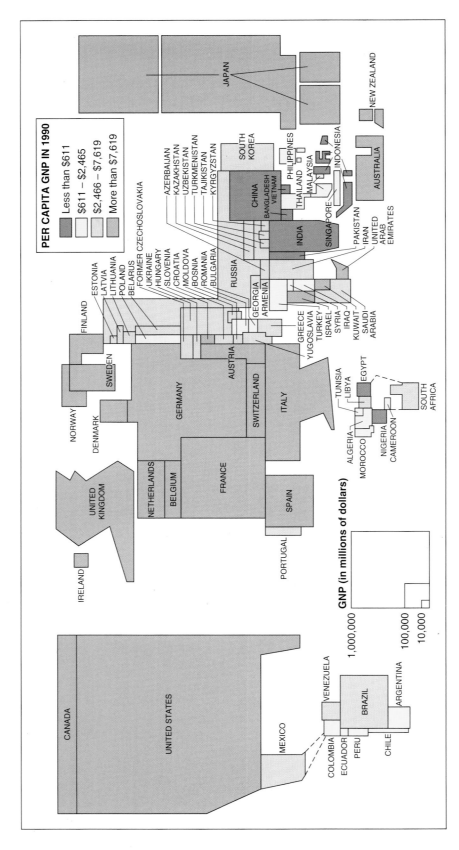

In a *cartogram* such as this, the size of countries is shown in proportion to some quantitative value, in this instance their total gross national product, or GNP. Note that many smaller countries are not shown in the cartogram. If they were, you would need a magnifying glass to find them! The color values represent per capita GNP, a particularly good measure of relative levels of economic development and illustrates the vast differences in wealth that separate the poorest countries from the richest. A small number of countries possess most of the world's wealth. Compare this cartogram with that of Map 20, which shows population size and growth rates for the world's countries. Note how the smaller countries in the map above tend to be larger in Map 20.

A word of caution: GNP should not be used as the only yardstick of economic development, because it does not measure the distribution of wealth among a population. There are countries (most notably, the oil-rich countries of the Middle East) where per capita GNP is high but where the bulk of the wealth is concentrated in the hands of a few individuals, leaving the remainder in poverty. Even within wealthy countries such as the United States there is an uneven distribution of wealth. A few countries (such as Costa Rica and Sri Lanka) have relatively low per capita GNPs, but rank relatively high in other measures of human well-being like average life expectancy, access to medical care, and literacy.

– 28 –

Map 14 Economic Output Per Sector

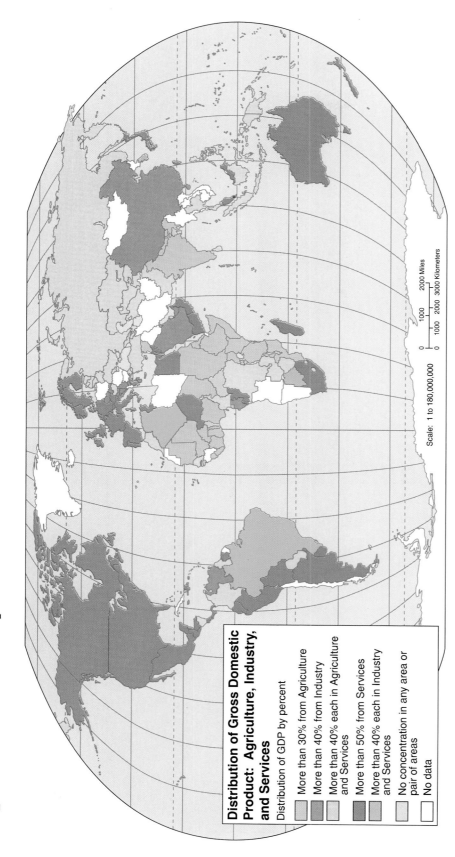

Distribution of Gross Domestic Product: Agriculture, Industry, and Services

Distribution of GDP by percent

- More than 30% from Agriculture
- More than 40% from Industry
- More than 40% each in Agriculture and Services
- More than 50% from Services
- More than 40% each in Industry and Services
- No concentration in any area or pair of areas
- No data

Scale: 1 to 180,000,000

0   1000   2000 Miles
0   1000   2000   3000 Kilometers

The percentage of the gross domestic product (the final output of goods and services produced by the domestic economy, including net exports of goods and nonfactor—non-labor, non-capital—services) that is devoted to agricultural, industrial, and service activities is thought to be a good measure of the level of economic development. In general, countries with more than 30 percent of their GDP derived from agriculture are still countries in a "colonial dependency" economy—that is, they are raising agricultural goods primarily for the export market and are dependent upon that market (usually the richer countries). Similarly, countries with more than 30 percent of GDP based on agriculture and 40 percent or more based on services are countries with active resource extractive (primarily mining and forestry) activities. These also

tend to be "colonial dependency" countries, providing raw materials for a foreign market. Countries with more than 40 percent of their GDP obtained from industry are normally countries that are well along the path to economic development. Countries with more than half of their GDP based on service activities fall into two ends of the development spectrum. On the one hand are countries heavily dependent upon extractive activities, tourism, and other low-level service functions. On the other hand are countries that can properly be termed "post-industrial": they have already passed through the industrial stage of their economic development and now rely less on the manufacture of products than on finance, research, communication, education, and other service-oriented economies.

– 29 –

Map 15 Employment by Sector

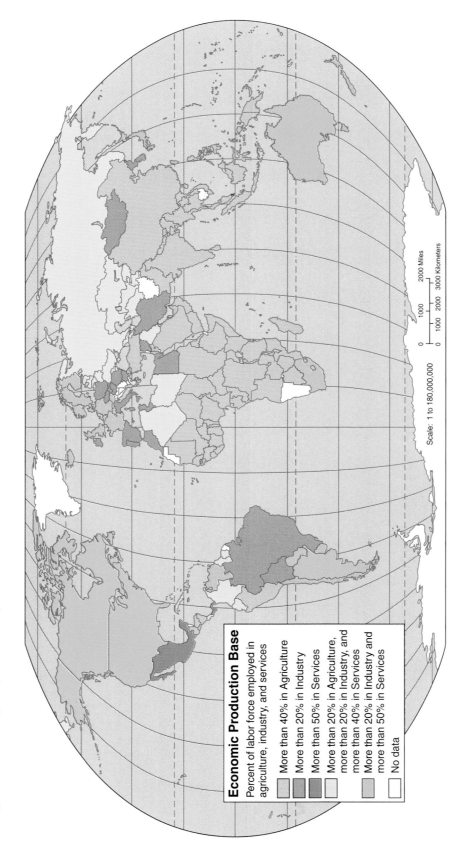

Economic Production Base

Percent of labor force employed in agriculture, industry, and services

- More than 40% in Agriculture
- More than 20% in Industry
- More than 50% in Services
- More than 20% in Agriculture, more than 20% in Industry, and more than 40% in Services
- More than 20% in Industry and more than 50% in Services
- No data

Scale: 1 to 180,000,000

```
0        1000         2000 Miles
0   1000   2000   3000 Kilometers
```

The employment structure of a country's population is one of the best indicators of the country's position on the scale of economic development. At one end of the scale are those countries with more than 40 percent of their labor force employed in agriculture. These are almost invariably the least developed, with high population growth rates, poor human services, significant environmental problems, and so on. In the middle of the scale are three types of countries: those with more than 20 percent of their labor force employed in industry and a fairly even balance in other sectors, those with more than 50 percent in services but with low industrial employment, and those with a fairly even balance among agricultural, industrial, and service employment. These are mostly countries that have undergone the industrial revolution fairly re-

cently and are still developing an industrial base while building up their service activities. They also include countries with a disproportionate share of their economies in service activities, where those service activities are primarily related to resource extraction. On the other end of the scale from the lesser developed economies are those countries that have more than 50 percent of their labor force employed in service activities and more than 20 percent employed in industry. These countries are, for the most part, those with a highly developed, automated industrial base and a highly mechanized agricultural system ("post-industrial" countries). They also include, particularly where they are found in Latin America and Africa, industrializing countries that are also heavily engaged in resource extraction as a service activity.

Map 16 Per Capita Income

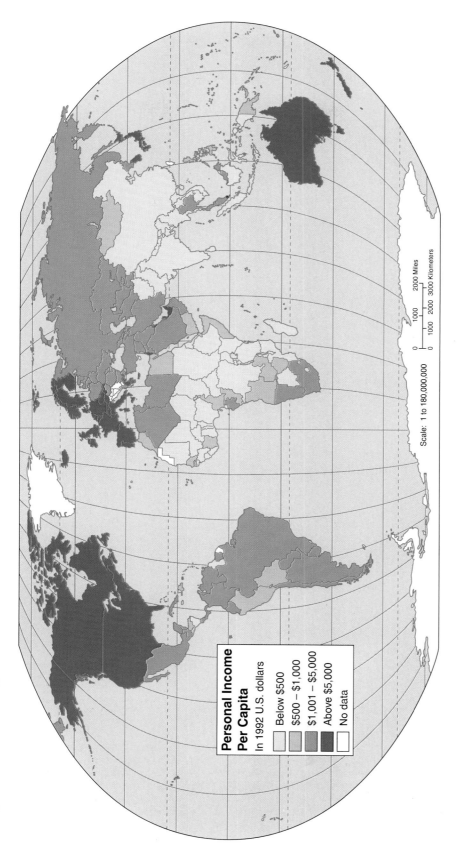

Personal Income Per Capita

In 1992 U.S. dollars

- Below $500
- $500 – $1,000
- $1,001 – $5,000
- Above $5,000
- No data

Scale: 1 to 180,000,000

0   1000   2000 Miles
0   1000   2000   3000 Kilometers

Of all the economic measures that separate the "haves" from the "have-nots," perhaps per capita income is the most meaningful. While there are distortions in per capita figures—for example, in those countries where mineral wealth makes a few enormously wealthy, thus driving up the per capita figures—generally per capita income provides a valid measurement of the ability of a country's population to provide for itself the things that those of us in the developed nations take for granted: adequate food, shelter, clothing, education, and ac-

cess to medical care. A glance at the map shows a clear-cut demarcation between temperate and tropical zones, with most of the countries with per capita incomes above $5,000 in the mid-latitude zones and most of those with lower per capita incomes in the tropical and equatorial regions. Where exceptions to this generalization occur, they are usually explainable in terms of tremendous maldistribution of wealth among a country's population.

Map 17 Central Government Expenditures Per Capita

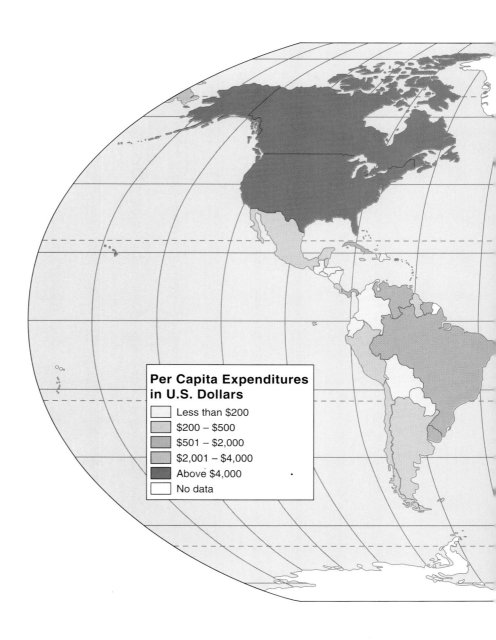

Per Capita Expenditures in U.S. Dollars

- Less than $200
- $200 – $500
- $501 – $2,000
- $2,001 – $4,000
- Above $4,000
- No data

The amount of money that the central government of a country spends upon a variety of essential governmental functions is a relative measure of economic development, particularly when it is viewed on a per person basis. These expenditures are devoted to such governmental responsibilities as agriculture, communication, culture, defense, education, fishing and hunting, health, housing, recreation, religion, social security, transportation, and welfare. Generally, the higher the level of economic development, the greater the per capita expenditures on these services. However, the data do mask some internal variations. For example, countries that tend to spend 20 percent or more

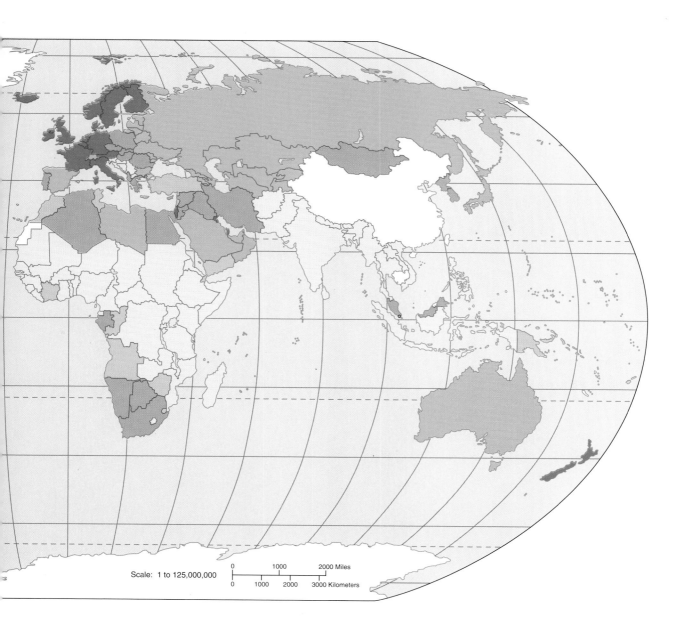

of their central government expenditures on defense will often show up as being in the more developed category when, in fact, all the figures really show is that a disproportionate amount of the money available to the government is devoted to purchasing armaments and maintaining a large standing military force. Thus, the fact that Libya spends $2,867 per capita—nearly 10 times the average for Africa—does not suggest that the average Libyan is 10 times better off than the average Tanzanian. Nevertheless, this map—particularly when compared with Map 34—does provide a reasonable approximation of economic development levels.

Map 18 International Trade Base

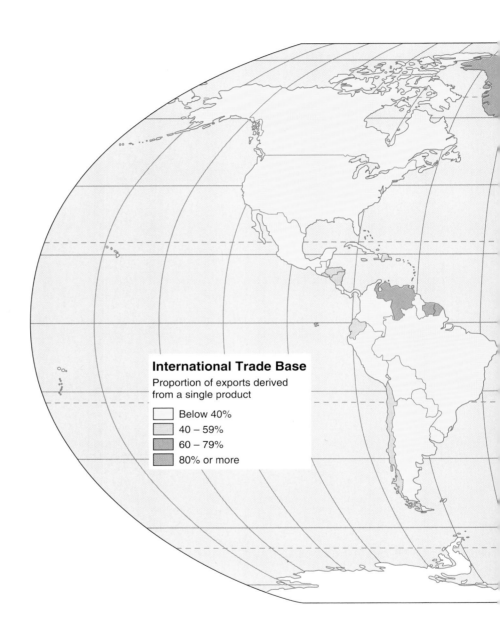

International Trade Base

Proportion of exports derived from a single product

- Below 40%
- 40 – 59%
- 60 – 79%
- 80% or more

It is an axiom in international economics that the more products a country exports, the stronger its economy is. One need only look at the export market for Japanese products and the relative strength of the Japanese economy to verify that axiom. Conversely, those countries with limited numbers of products to export are hampered in their economic growth. A country with only one or two products upon which its export revenues are dependent is vulnerable to economic shifts, particularly the changing

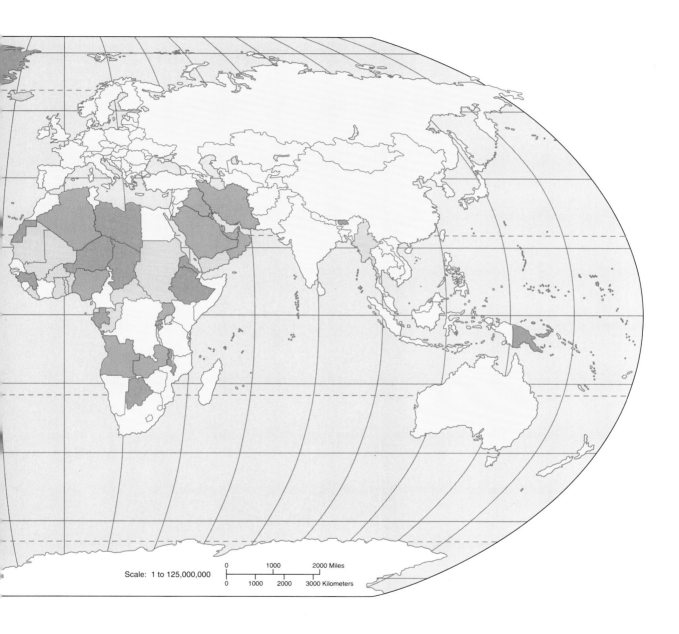

market demand for its products. Imagine what would happen to the thriving economic status of the oil-exporting states of the Persian Gulf, for example, should an alternate source of cheap energy be found. A glance at this map shows that, generally, those countries with the lowest levels of economic development tend to export primarily one or two products and, therefore, have economies that are especially vulnerable to economic instabilities.

Map 19 Dependence on Trade

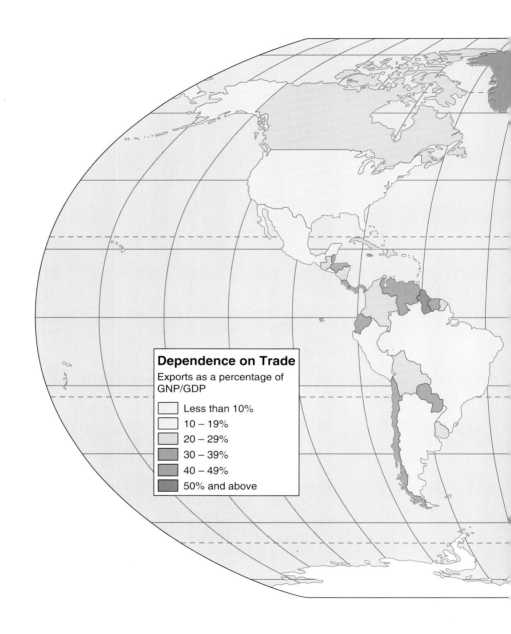

Dependence on Trade

Exports as a percentage of GNP/GDP

- Less than 10%
- 10 – 19%
- 20 – 29%
- 30 – 39%
- 40 – 49%
- 50% and above

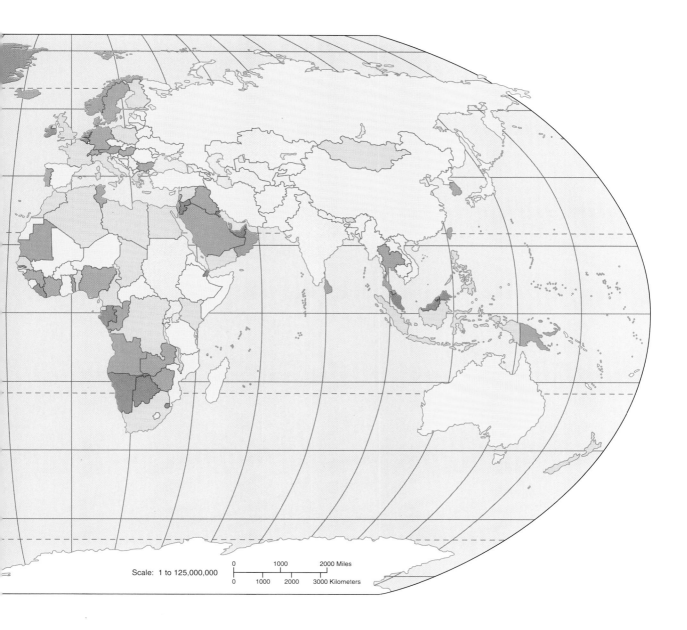

As the global economy becomes more and more a reality, the economic strength of virtually all countries is increasingly dependent on trade. Even countries like the United States, Japan, and Germany, with huge and diverse economies, depend on exports to generate a significant percentage of their employment and wealth. For many developing nations with relatively abundant resources and limited industrial capacity, exports provide the primary base upon which their economy rests. Without imports, many products we desire would be unavailable or more expensive; without exports, many jobs would be eliminated.

Table C
World Countries: Basic Economic Indicators

COUNTRIES	GROSS NATIONAL PRODUCT (GNP)		AVERAGE ANNUAL CHANGE IN GNP		DISTRIBUTION OF GROSS DOMESTIC PRODUCT (%)[1]		
	TOTAL (millions of $)	PER CAPITA ($)	1979 (%)	1989 (%)	AGRICULTURE	INDUSTRY	SERVICES
AFRICA							
Algeria	53,116	2,170	6.4	3.3	13.2	43.2	43.6
Angola	6,010	620	X[2]	X	X	X	X
Benin	1,753	380	2.4	2.3	45.5	12.1	42.4
Botswana	1,105	940	13.5	10.8	2.9	54.8	42.3
Burkina Faso	2,176	310	3.2	3.8	31.8	24.3	43.8
Burundi	1,149	220	8.9	4.2	55.9	15.0	29.1
Cameroon	11,661	1,010	6.1	4.4	27.0	27.9	45.1
Cape Verde	281	760	X	8.9	14.4	17.1	68.5
Central African Republic	1,144	390	2.3	0.5	42.2	15.3	42.5
Chad	1,038	190	-1.5	4.7	35.8	20.0	44.2
Comoros	209	460	2.1	4.5	35.8	14.1	50.1
Congo	2,045	930	5.4	6.1	13.7	35.5	50.8
Djibouti	333	1,070	X	X	X	X	X
Egypt	32,501	630	7.1	5.6	21.2	25.0	53.9
Equatorial Guinea	149	430	X	X	58.7	10.3	31.0
Ethiopia	5,953	120	3.2	2.4	43.1	16.8	40.1
Gabon	3,060	2,770	8.0	0.8	10.3	46.5	43.2
Gambia	196	230	5.3	2.3	34.1	10.3	55.6
Ghana	5,503	380	1.5	1.9	50.2	17.9	31.8
Guinea	2,372	430	X	X	X	X	X
Guinea-Bissau	173	180	X	2.4	47.0	15.8	37.2
Ivory Coast	9,305	790	6.3	1.2	46.0	24.0	30.0
Kenya	8,785	380	7.1	4.2	30.7	19.5	49.8
Lesotho	816	470	12.4	2.0	24.0	29.8	46.2
Liberia	1,052	450	3.3	X	37.0	28.0	35.0
Libya	22,976	5,410	3.4	-4.7	X	X	X
Madagascar	2,543	230	1.6	-0.5	31.4	14.4	54.2
Malawi	1,475	180	6.0	2.2	34.8	20.1	45.1
Mali	2,109	260	5.1	3.4	49.6	12.2	38.2
Mauritania	953	490	2.1	1.6	37.6	24.1	38.3
Mauritius	2,068	1,950	6.4	4.2	12.6	32.0	55.3
Morocco	22,069	900	5.0	3.9	15.5	35.7	48.8
Mozambique	1,193	80	X	X	64.4	22.0	13.6
Namibia	1,540	1,245	X	X	X	X	X
Niger	2,195	1,245	1.5	-0.6	36.4	12.6	51.0
Nigeria	28.134	250	6.3	-0.1	30.7	44.1	25.2
Rwanda	2,157	310	4.5	2.2	37.1	22.8	40.1
Senegal	4,176	650	2.8	2.2	22.0	31.1	46.9
Sierra Leone	813	200	2.2	1.8	46.3	12.4	41.3
Somalia	1,035	170	4.7	1.2	64.8	9.6	25.7
South Africa	86,029	2,460	3.4	2.2	5.8	43.9	50.3
Sudan	13,225	540	4.1	1.7	36.0	14.6	49.4
Swaziland	683	900	5.6	4.0	23.2	40.3	36.5
Tanzania	3,079	120	3.8	1.8	65.6	7.5	26.9
Togo	1,364	390	3.3	2.0	33.9	22.6	43.6
Tunisia	10,089	1,260	7.2	3.6	13.8	32.8	53.4
Uganda	4,254	250	-1.8	2.7	72.5	7.4	20.2
Zaire	8.841	260	-0.1	1.6	29.6	32.1	38.3
Zambia	3,060	390	1.4	1.5	14.2	43.0	42.8
Zimbabwe	6,076	640	4.9	4.3	12.7	38.8	48.5
NORTH AND CENTRAL AMERICA							
Barbados	1,622	6,370	3.4	1.5	6.6	20.9	72.5
Belize	294	1,600	6.4	4.1	22.7	22.6	54.7
Canada	500,337	19,020	6.9	2.9	3.3	34.8	61.8
Costa Rica	4,898	1,790	6.1	1.6	17.8	26.7	55.4

(continued on next page)

COUNTRIES	GROSS NATIONAL PRODUCT (GNP)		AVERAGE ANNUAL CHANGE IN GNP		DISTRIBUTION OF GROSS DOMESTIC PRODUCT (%)[1]		
	TOTAL (millions of $)	PER CAPITA ($)	1979 (%)	1989 (%)	AGRICULTURE	INDUSTRY	SERVICES
Cuba	20,900	2,000	X	X	X	X	X
Dominican Republic	5,513	790	7.6	2.3	15.2	25.5	59.3
El Salvador	5,356	1,040	4.5	-1.2	21.5	23.1	55.4
Guatemala	8,205	920	6.0	0.8	X	X	X
Haiti	2,556	400	3.5	0.0	31.3	38.0	30.7
Honduras	4,495	900	5.6	2.1	20.6	25.1	54.3
Jamaica	3,011	1,260	0.6	0.5	5.6	42.0	52.4
Mexico	170,053	1,990	9.2	2.0	8.0	32.2	59.8
Nicaragua	2,803	800	-0.4	-2.0	21.0	34.0	46.0
Panama	4,211	1,780	4.9	0.7	10.2	14.9	74.9
Trinidad and Tobago	4,000	3.160	4.5	-3.4	2.8	39.7	57.4
United States	5,237,707	21,100	2.8	2.6	2.0	29.3	68.7
SOUTH AMERICA							
Argentina	68,780	2,160	2.9	-1.6	13.8	32.7	53.5
Bolivia	4,301	600	3.9	-0.4	24.0	27.0	49.0
Brazil	375,146	2,550	8.4	2.7	8.6	42.9	48.5
Chile	22,910	1,770	2.0	3.2	X	X	X
Colombia	38,607	1,190	6.0	3.0	16.8	36.4	46.8
Ecuador	10,774	1,040	9.4	2.3	16.0	31.0	53.0
Guyana	248	340	2.3	-2.3	24.5	31.2	44.3
Paraguay	4,299	1,030	8.1	3.6	29.5	22.4	48.1
Peru	23,009	1,090	3.5	0.1	7.6	30.5	61.9
Suriname	1,314	3.020	4.7	-2.1	11.0	25.8	63.3
Uruguay	8.069	2,620	2.6	-0.2	10.8	28.2	61.0
Venezuela	47,164	2,450	4.5	-0.8	6.1	45.8	48.1
ASIA							
Afghanistan	X	X	X	X	X	X	X
Bahrain	3,009	6,360	X	X	1.2	43.1	55.7
Bangladesh	19,913	180	2.4	3.5	44.3	14.4	41.3
Bhutan	266	190	X	X	46.1	29.3	24.6
Cambodia	X	X	X	X	X	X	X
China	393,006	360	7.4	8.9	32.4	46.1	21.4
Cyprus	4,892	7,050	X	5.9	7.1	26.9	66.0
India	287,383	350	3.0	5.6	31.7	28.5	39.8
Indonesia	87,936	490	7.1	6.5	24.1	35.7	40.2
Iran	97,600	1,800	5.0	1.7	X	X	X
Iraq	35,000	1,940	X	X	X	X	X
Israel	44,131	9.750	5.6	3.6	X	X	X
Japan	2,920,310	23,730	5.3	4.1	2.6	41.2	56.2
Jordan	5,291	1,730	X	X	5.9	28.0	66.1
Korea, North	28,000	1,240	X	X	X	X	X
Korea, South	186,467	4,400	9.6	8.1	10.2	44.0	45.8
Kuwait	33,082	16,380	5.3	-0.8	1.0	55.6	43.4
Laos	693	170	X	X	X	X	X
Lebanon	X	X	X	X	X	X	X
Malaysia	37,005	2,130	7.5	5.7	X	X	X
Mongolia	X	X	X	X	X	X	X
Myanmar	X	X	4.5	2.3	X	X	X
Nepal	3,206	170	2.6	4.0	58.7	15.0	26.4
Oman	7,756	5,220	7.4	9.2	3.0	43.0	57.0
Pakistan	40,134	370	4.7	6.8	26.6	23.9	49.5
Philippines	34,427	700	6.3	1.8	23.5	33.3	43.3
Qatar	4,077	9,920	X	-0.4	X	X	X
Saudi Arabia	89,986	6,230	13.3	0.5	7.6	42.8	49.6
Singapore	28,058	10,450	9.0	7.2	0.3	37.1	62.6
Sri Lanka	7,268	430	4.4	4.0	26.0	26.8	47.2
Syria	12,812	1,100	8.5	2.4	38.3	16.0	45.6
Thailand	64,437	1,170	7.0	7.3	16.9	35.1	48.0
Turkey	74,731	1,360	5.7	4.3	16.5	35.6	47.9

(continued on next page)

COUNTRIES	GROSS NATIONAL PRODUCT (GNP)		AVERAGE ANNUAL CHANGE IN GNP		DISTRIBUTION OF GROSS DOMESTIC PRODUCT (%)[1]		
	TOTAL (millions of $)	PER CAPITA ($)	1979 (%)	1989 (%)	AGRICULTURE	INDUSTRY	SERVICES
United Arab Emirates	28,449	18,430	X	-0.4	1.7	55.4	42.9
Vietnam	14,200	215	X	X	X	X	X
Yemen	8,403	711	X	X	25.0	20.0	55.0
EUROPE							
Albania	3,800	1,200	X	X	X	X	X
Austria	117,341	17,360	3.9	2.1	3.2	37.0	59.8
Belgium	162,026	16,390	X	X	2.0	30.8	67.2
Bulgaria	20,860	2,320	X	X	X	X	X
Czechoslo-vakia[3]	123,200	7,878	X	X	X	X	X
Denmark	105,262	20,510	2.3	1.4	4.9	28.9	66.3
Finland	109,705	22.060	3.7	3.6	6.5	35.4	58.1
France	1,000,866	17,830	3.4	2.1	3.3	29.3	67.3
Germany	1,432,459	20,948	3.1	1.9	1.5	40.1	58.4
Greece	53,626	5,340	5.3	1.2	16.2	29.2	54.6
Hungary	27,078	2,560	X	1.1	14.4	36.9	48.7
Iceland	5,351	21,240	6.4	2.4	X	X	X
Ireland	30,054	8.500	4.3	1.4	9.9	37.4	52.7
Italy	871,955	15,150	3.8	2.4	3.7	33.7	62.7
Luxembourg	9,408	24,860	7.8	4.5	2.3	35.2	62.5
Malta	2,041	5,820	10.7	3.7	3.9	40.5	55.6
Netherlands	237,415	16,010	3.3	1.5	4.0	30.7	65.3
Norway	72,028	21,850	4.2	3.5	3.0	34.0	63.0
Poland	66,974	1,760	X	X	X	X	X
Portugal	44,058	4,260	4.9	2.9	8.7	37.1	54.2
Romania	79,800	3,445	X	1.6	X	X	X
Spain	358,352	9,150	3.8	2.8	6.2	36.8	57.0
Sweden	184,230	21,170	2.4	1.8	3.3	34.8	61.9
Switzerland	197,984	30,270	6.8	2.4	X	X	X
United Kingdom	834,166	14,570	2.8	2.0	1.8	37.9	60.3
U.S.S.R.[4]	2,659,500	9,211	X	X	X	X	X
Yugoslavia[5]	59,080	2,490	6.1	0.3	13.8	49.4	36.8
OCEANIA							
Australia	242,131	14,440	3.5	3.0	4.2	31.5	64.3
Fiji	1,218	1,640	6.8	0.7	23.7	20.9	55.4
New Zealand	39,437	11,800	1.6	1.8	8.4	28.0	63.6
Papua New Guinea	3,444	900	3.7	1.2	28.4	30.6	41.0
Solomon Islands	181	570	X	4.9	X	X	X

[1]The distribution of Gross Domestic Product may not add up to 100 percent due to rounding of percentages.

[2]Throughout the Atlas, the letter X indicates that no data are available for that particular country. In some cases, this represents withholding of data that may be considered to have some military or defense significance if it were released. More frequently, the country simply does not collect the data. In some unusual circumstances, the absence of data can be taken to mean that the particular information does not pertain to the country.

[3]On January 1, 1993, Czechoslovakia was separated by peaceful agreement into two independent countries, the Czech Republic and the Slovak Republic. At the time of this printing, information was not yet available for these two separate countries.

[4]At the time of this printing, separate statistical data on the countries of the Commonwealth of Independent States were not yet available, nor were there available data on the former Soviet republics that are not members of the C.I.S. The data for the former U.S.S.R. thus include information for Russia and the other Commonwealth countries of Armenia, Azerbaijan, Belarus, Kazakhstan, Kyrgyzstan, Moldova, Tajikistan, Turkmenistan, Ukraine, and Uzbekistan, along with the non-Commonwealth countries of Estonia, Georgia, Latvia, and Lithuania.

[5]At the time of this printing, separate statistical data on the countries that made up the former state of Yugoslavia were not yet available. The data for Yugoslavia thus include information for the Federal Republic of Yugoslavia (Serbia and Montenegro) and the independent countries of Bosnia-Herzegovina, Croatia, Macedonia, and Slovenia.

Sources: The World Bank; Organization for Economic Cooperation and Development; U.S. Central Intelligence Agency; *World Resources 1992–93.*

Part IV

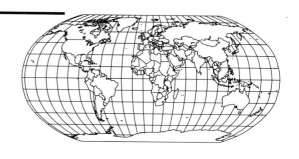

Population and Human Development

Map 20 Population Size and Growth Rate

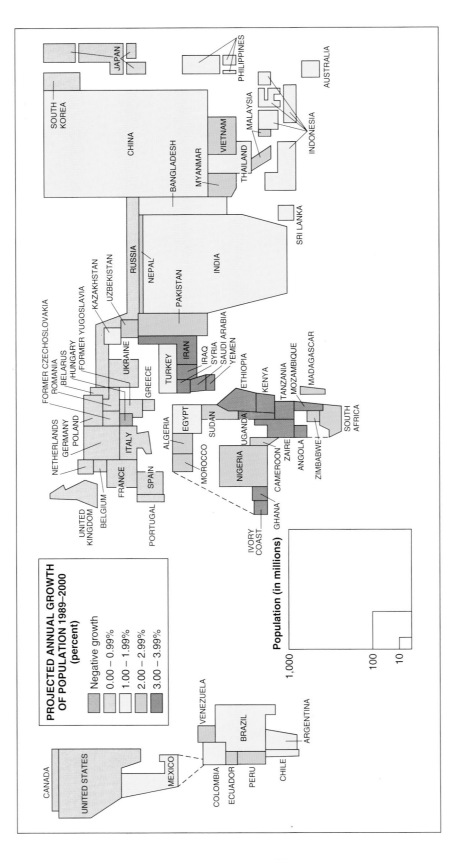

The sizes of countries in this cartogram are in direct proportion to their total populations. Thus, although the actual land areas of China and the United States are about the same, China appears about four times larger than the United States in the cartogram because its population is approximately four times that of the United States. In addition to showing the relative sizes of the population of countries, the cartogram also uses different colors to show population growth rates for all countries. It is apparent from the cartogram that some of the countries with the largest populations (such as India) also have high growth rates. Since these countries tend to be in developing regions, the combination of high population and high growth rates poses special problems for continuing economic development and for preventing environmental degradation. The average global population increase is about 1.7 percent, which means that the world population will double in approximately 30 years. But for many countries in Latin America, Africa, and Asia, population growth rates are well in excess of that global average (often more than 3 percent), with doubling times of less than 20 years. These rapidly expanding populations place enormous burdens upon the economic, social, and political structures of their countries, which many people believe may cause environmental and human disaster as early as the middle of the twenty-first century.

PROJECTED ANNUAL GROWTH OF POPULATION 1989–2000 (percent)

- Negative growth
- 0.00 – 0.99%
- 1.00 – 1.99%
- 2.00 – 2.99%
- 3.00 – 3.99%

Population (in millions)

1,000

100

10

Map 21 Infant Mortality

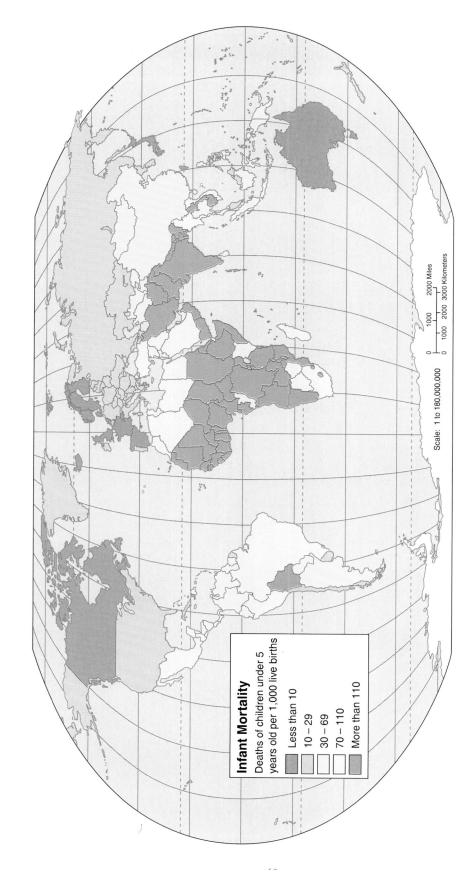

Infant Mortality

Deaths of children under 5
years old per 1,000 live births

- Less than 10
- 10 – 29
- 30 – 69
- 70 – 110
- More than 110

Scale: 1 to 180,000,000

| 0 | 1000 | 2000 Miles |

| 0 | 1000 | 2000 | 3000 Kilometers |

Infant mortality rates are calculated by dividing the number of children born in a given year who die before their fifth birthday by the number of children born in the same year, and then multiplying by 1,000. Infant mortality rates are prime indicators of economic development. In highly developed economies, with advanced medical technologies, sufficient diet, adequate public sanitation, and so on, the infant mortality rates tend to be quite low. In less developed countries, however, where the disadvantages of poor diet, limited access to medical technology, and the other problems of poverty exist, infant mortality rates tend to be high. Although reductions in infant mortality rates have occurred worldwide during the last two decades, many regions of the world still experience rates above the 10 percent level. Such infant mortality rates not only represent human tragedy at its most basic level; they are also are powerful inhibiting factors for the future of human development. Compare the differences in the North and in the South. Parents in most African countries witness the death of their children at a rate more than 10 times higher than parents in some Northern countries, such as Canada.

Map 22 Average Life Expectancy at Birth

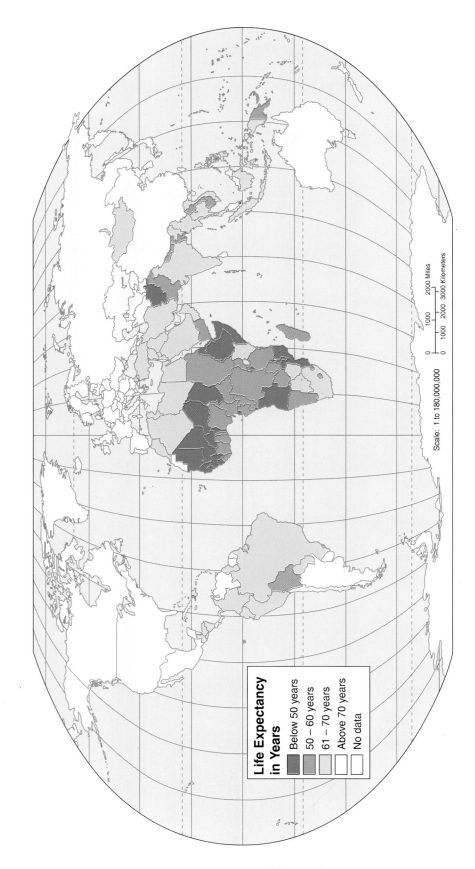

Life Expectancy in Years

- Below 50 years
- 50 – 60 years
- 61 – 70 years
- Above 70 years
- No data

Scale: 1 to 180,000,000

0   1000   2000 Miles

0   1000   2000   3000 Kilometers

Average life expectancy at birth is a measure of the average longevity of the population of a country. Like all average measures, it is distorted by extremes. For example, a country with a high mortality rate among children will have a low average life expectancy. Thus, an average life expectancy of 45 years does not mean that everyone can be expected to die at the age of 45. Usually what the figure means is that a substantial number of children between birth and 5 years of age die, thus reducing the average life expectancy for the

entire population. In spite of the dangers inherent in misinterpreting the data, average life expectancy (along with infant mortality and several other measures) is a valid way of judging the relative health of a population. It reflects the nature of the health care system, of public sanitation and disease control, of nutrition, and a number of other key human need indicators. As such, it is a measure of "well-being" that is significant in indicating economic development.

Map 23 Population by Age Group

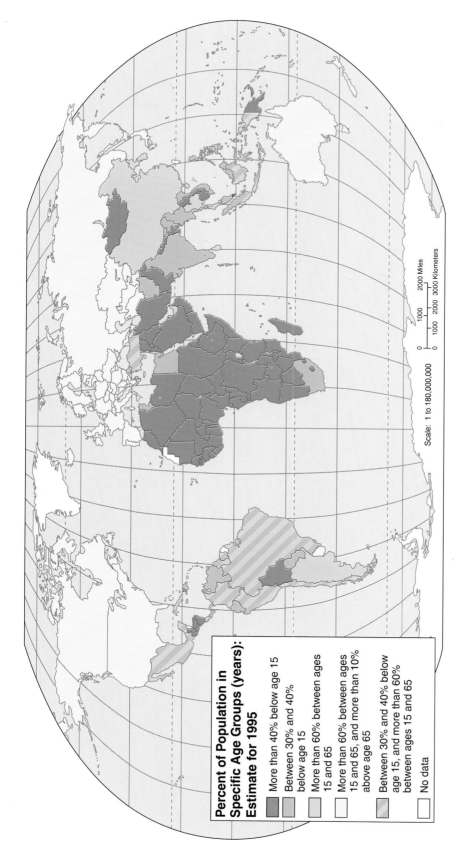

Percent of Population in Specific Age Groups (years): Estimate for 1995

- More than 40% below age 15
- Between 30% and 40% below age 15
- More than 60% between ages 15 and 65
- More than 60% between ages 15 and 65, and more than 10% above age 65
- Between 30% and 40% below age 15, and more than 60% between ages 15 and 65
- No data

Scale: 1 to 180,000,000

0   1000   2000 Miles
0   1000   2000   3000 Kilometers

Of all the measurements that illustrate the dynamics of a population, age distribution may be the most significant, particularly when viewed in combination with average population growth rates. The particular relevance of age distribution is that it tells us what to expect from a population in terms of growth over the next generation. If, for example, approximately somewhere between 40 percent and 50 percent of a population is below the age of 15, that suggests that in the next generation about one-quarter of the total population will be women of childbearing age. When age distribution is combined with fertility rates (the average number of children born per woman in a population), an especially valid measurement of future growth potential may be derived. A simple example: Nigeria, with a 1990 population of 109 million, has 50 percent of its population below the age of 15 and a fertility rate of 6.6; the United States, with a 1990 population of 250 million, has 21 percent of its population below the age of 15 and a fertility rate of 1.9. During the period in which those women presently under the age of 15 are in their childbearing years, Nigeria can be expected to add a total of approximately 180 million persons to its total population. Over the same period, the United States can be expected to add only 50 million.

Map 24 Total Labor Force

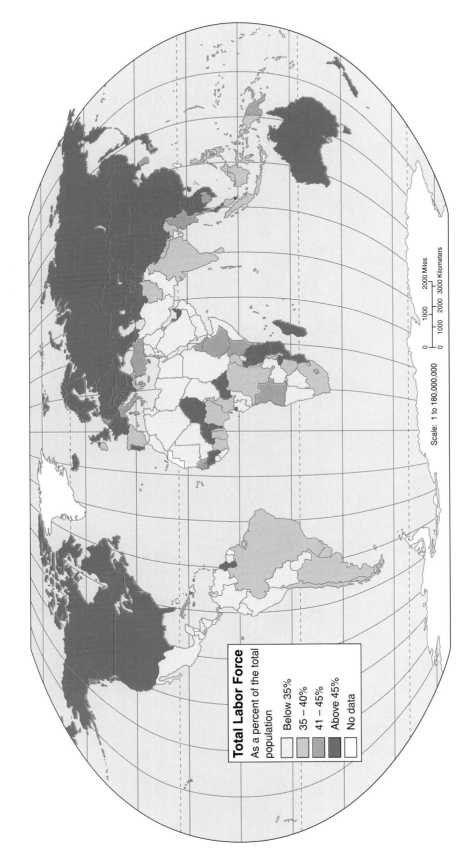

Total Labor Force

As a percent of the total population

- Below 35%
- 35 – 40%
- 41 – 45%
- Above 45%
- No data

Scale: 1 to 180,000,000

0   1000   2000 Miles

0   1000   2000   3000 Kilometers

The term *labor force* refers to the economically active portion of a population, that is, all people who work or are without work but are available for and are seeking work to produce economic goods and services. The total labor force thus includes both employed and unemployed (as long as they are actively seeking employment). Labor force is considered to be a better indicator of economic potential than employment/unemployment figures, since unemployment figures will contain experienced workers with considerable potential who are temporarily out of work. Unemployment figures will also include per-

sons seeking employment for the first time (recent college graduates, for example). Generally, countries with higher percentages of total population within the labor force will be countries with higher levels of economic development. This is partly a function of levels of education and training and partly a function of the age distribution of populations, with substantially larger percentages of populations in developing countries being too young to be part of the labor force.

Map 25 Urban Population as Percentage of Total

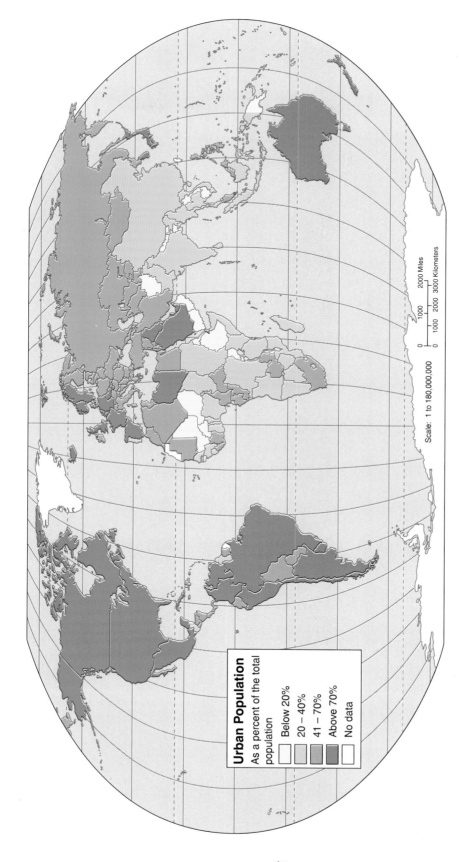

Urban Population

As a percent of the total population

- Below 20%
- 20 – 40%
- 41 – 70%
- Above 70%
- No data

Scale: 1 to 180,000,000

2000 Miles

3000 Kilometers

The proportion of a country's population that resides in urban areas was formerly considered to be a measure of relative economic development, with countries possessing a large urban population ranking high on the development scale and vice versa. Given the rapid rate of urbanization in developing countries, however, this traditional measure is no longer as valuable. What relative urbanization rates now tell us is something about levels of economic development in a negative sense. Latin American, African, and Asian countries with more than 40 percent of their populations living in urban areas are countries that are quite probably suffering from a variety of problems: rural overpopulation and flight from the land, urban poverty and despair, high unemployment, and poor public services. The rate of urbanization in the Third World is such that many cities in developing nations may outstrip those in North America and Europe by the end of this century. It has been estimated, for example, that Mexico City may have as many as 44 million inhabitants by the year 2000. Far from being a picture of economic health, as we once viewed urbanization, this is a picture of potential economic and environmental disaster.

Table D

World Countries: Average Annual Population Growth (%), 1980–2000

COUNTRIES	1980	1990	2000
WORLD	**1.73**	**1.74**	**1.63**
AFRICA	**2.88**	**2.98**	**2.99**
Algeria	3.14	2.72	2.73
Angola	3.39	2.70	2.85
Benin	2.63	3.00	3.23
Botswana	3.54	3.71	3.24
Burkina Faso	2.30	2.66	3.02
Burundi	2.32	2.91	2.91
Cameroon	2.81	3.27	3.48
Cape Verde	0.80	2.65	3.21
Central African Republic	2.41	2.77	2.98
Chad	2.10	2.47	2.58
Comoros	4.06	3.45	3.63
Congo	2.85	3.16	3.35
Djibouti	4.49	2.88	3.05
Egypt	2.38	2.39	1.90
Equatorial Guinea	-.71	2.42	2.60
Ethiopia	2.44	2.67	2.99
Gabon	4.70	3.47	3.09
Gambia	3.15	2.89	2.58
Ghana	1.76	3.15	3.10
Guinea	1.45	2.86	3.12
Guinea-Bissau	4.74	1.99	2.20
Ivory Coast	3.86	3.78	3.83
Kenya	3.82	3.58	3.81
Lesotho	2.41	2.85	2.87
Liberia	3.02	3.16	3.30
Libya	4.37	3.65	3.54
Madagascar	2.91	3.18	3.28
Malawi	3.29	3.53	3.43
Mali	2.13	3.04	3.22
Mauritania	2.46	2.73	2.92
Mauritius	1.59	1.17	1.01
Morocco	2.27	2.58	2.18
Mozambique	2.83	2.65	2.68
Namibia	2.70	3.19	3.17
Niger	3.15	3.14	3.33
Nigeria	3.35	3.30	3.17
Rwanda	3.27	3.41	3.41
Senegal	2.84	2.78	2.86
Sierra Leone	2.15	2.49	2.75
Somalia	5.03	3.26	2.85
South Africa	2.22	2.22	2.08
Sudan	3.08	2.88	2.87
Swaziland	3.12	3.44	3.47
Tanzania	3.42	3.66	3.66
Togo	2.70	3.07	3.22
Tunisia	2.58	2.38	1.79
Uganda	3.20	3.67	3.47
Zaire	2.86	3.14	3.25
Zambia	3.40	3.75	3.65
Zimbabwe	2.97	3.16	2.92
NORTH AND CENTRAL AMERICA	**1.47**	**1.29**	**1.09**
Barbados	0.28	O.16	O.45
Belize	2.50	2.39	1.92
Canada	1.13	0.88	0.66
Costa Rica	2.98	2.64	1.90
Cuba	0.79	1.03	0.73
Dominican Republic	2.42	2.22	1.71
El Salvador	2.05	1.93	2.51
Guatemala	2.77	2.88	2.81
Haiti	1.68	2.01	2.07
Honduras	3.46	3.18	2.75
Jamaica	1.16	1.21	0.99
Mexico	2.57	2.20	1.81
Nicaragua	2.81	3.36	2.95
Panama	2.26	2.07	1.69
Trinidad and Tobago	1.33	1.68	1.51
United States	1.06	0.81	0.60
SOUTH AMERICA	**2.28**	**2.01**	**1.71**
Argentina	1.61	1.27	1.12
Bolivia	2.59	2.76	2.88
Brazil	2.31	2.07	1.67
Chile	1.48	1.66	1.40
Colombia	2.29	1.97	1.70
Ecuador	2.88	2.56	2.20
Guyana	0.68	0.15	1.44
Paraguay	3.20	2.93	2.48
Peru	2.63	2.08	1.93
Suriname	-0.70	1.94	1.52
Uruguay	0.59	0.56	0.55
Venezuela	3.42	2.61	2.14
ASIA	**1.86**	**1.87**	**1.68**
Afghanistan	0.87	2.63	2.74
Bahrain	4.88	3.67	2.54
Bangladesh	2.83	2.67	2.60
Bhutan	1.70	2.15	2.31
Cambodia	-2.07	2.48	1.75
China	1.43	1.45	1.22
Cyprus	0.65	1.04	0.77
India	2.08	2.07	1.91
Indonesia	2.14	1.93	1.60
Iran	3.08	2.74	2.60
Iraq	3.75	3.48	3.23
Israel	2.31	1.66	1.42
Japan	0.93	0.43	0.40
Jordan	2.34	3.25	3.19
Korea, North	1.95	1.81	1.72
Korea, South	1.55	0.95	0.77
Kuwait	6.24	3.40	2.34
Laos	1.16	2.82	2.64
Lebanon	-0.72	0.25	1.98
Malaysia	2.32	2.64	1.85
Mongolia	2.78	2.74	2.57
Myanmar	2.10	2.09	2.00
Nepal	2.67	2.48	2.25
Oman	5.01	3.79	3.67
Pakistan	2.64	3.44	2.75
Philippines	2.53	2.49	2.05
Qatar	5.84	4.16	2.70
Saudi Arabia	5.13	3.96	3.79
Singapore	1.30	1.25	0.84
Sri Lanka	1.71	1.33	1.14
Syria	3.36	3.61	3.45
Thailand	2.44	1.53	1.32
Turkey	2.09	2.08	1.63
United Arab Emirates	13.97	3.26	1.87

(continued on next page)

COUNTRIES	1980	1990	2000	COUNTRIES	1980	1990	2000
Vietnam	2.23	2.15	2.03	Malta	2.09	0.49	0.35
Yemen	3.50	3.76	3.56	Netherlands	0.71	0.63	0.54
				Norway	0.39	0.28	0.28
EUROPE	**0.45**	**0.25**	**0.23**	Poland	0.89	0.65	0.50
Albania	1.94	1.83	1.50	Portugal	1.43	0.25	0.30
Austria	-0.08	0.07	0.03	Romania	0.88	0.48	0.44
Belgium	0.11	-0.03	-0.03	Spain	1.06	0.30	0.37
Bulgaria	0.32	0.11	0.08	Sweden	0.29	0.22	0.12
Czechoslovakia[1]	0.68	0.21	0.38	Switzerland	-0.06	0.42	0.24
Denmark	0.25	0.08	-0.02	United Kingdom	0.04	0.22	0.18
Finland	0.29	0.30	0.18	U.S.S.R.[2]	0.85	0.78	0.64
France	0.44	0.35	0.35	Yugoslavia[3]	0.87	0.58	0.41
Germany	-0.09	0.10	-0.12				
Greece	1.28	0.23	0.14	**OCEANIA**	**1.49**	**1.48**	**1.24**
Hungary	0.34	-0.18	0.04	Australia	1.51	1.37	1.04
Iceland	0.91	0.97	0.73	Fiji	1.91	1.78	1.40
Ireland	1.36	0.92	0.93	New Zealand	0.19	0.87	0.71
Italy	0.35	-0.03	0.03	Papua New Guinea	2.46	2.26	2.20
Luxembourg	0.09	0.32	0.04	Solomon Islands	3.01	3.28	2.77

[1] On January 1, 1993, Czechoslovakia was separated by peaceful agreement into two independent countries, the Czech Republic and the Slovak Republic. At the time of this printing, information was not yet available for these two separate countries.

[2] At the time of this printing, separate statistical data on the countries of the Commonwealth of Independent States were not yet available, nor were there available data on the former Soviet republics that are not members of the C.I.S. The data for the former U.S.S.R. thus include information for Russia and the other Commonwealth countries of Armenia, Azerbaijan, Belarus, Kazakhstan, Kyrgyzstan, Moldova, Tajikistan, Turkmenistan, Ukraine, and Uzbekistan, along with the non-Commonwealth countries of Estonia, Georgia, Latvia, and Lithuania.

[3] At the time of this printing, separate statistical data on the countries that made up the former state of Yugoslavia were not yet available. The data for Yugoslavia thus include information for the Federal Republic of Yugoslavia (Serbia and Montenegro) and the independent countries of Bosnia-Herzegovina, Croatia, Macedonia, and Slovenia.

Sources: United Nations Population Division and International Labour Office; *World Resources 1992–93.*

Table E

World Countries: Total Fertility Rates,[1] 1975–1995

COUNTRIES	1970–1975	1990–1995
WORLD	**4.5**	**6.0**
AFRICA	**6.6**	**6.0**
Algeria	7.4	4.9
Angola	6.4	6.3
Benin	7.1	7.1
Botswana	6.9	6.4
Burkina Faso	6.7	6.5
Burundi	6.8	6.8
Cameroon	6.4	6.9
Cape Verde	7.0	5.3
Central African Republic	5.7	6.2
Chad	6.0	5.8
Comoros	7.0	7.0
Congo	6.3	6.3
Djibouti	6.6	6.5
Egypt	5.5	4.0
Equatorial Guinea	5.7	5.9
Ethiopia	6.8	6.8
Gabon	4.3	5.3
Gambia	6.5	6.2
Ghana	6.6	6.3
Guinea	7.0	7.0
Guinea-Bissau	5.4	5.8
Ivory Coast	7.4	7.4
Kenya	8.1	6.8
Lesotho	5.7	5.8
Liberia	6.8	6.7
Libya	7.6	6.7
Madagascar	6.6	6.5
Malawi	7.4	7.6
Mali	7.1	7.1
Mauritania	6.5	6.5
Mauritius	3.3	1.9
Morocco	6.9	4.2
Mozambique	6.5	6.2
Namibia	6.1	5.7
Niger	7.1	7.1
Nigeria	6.9	6.6
Rwanda	8.3	8.0
Senegal	7.0	6.2
Sierra Leone	6.5	6.5
Somalia	6.6	6.6
South Africa	5.5	4.2
Sudan	6.7	6.3
Swaziland	6.5	6.5
Tanzania	7.0	7.1
Togo	6.6	6.6
Tunisia	6.2	3.4
Uganda	7.0	7.3
Zaire	6.1	6.1
Zambia	6.9	7.2
Zimbabwe	7.2	5.3
NORTH AND CENTRAL AMERICA	**3.1**	**2.4**
Barbados	2.7	1.8
Belize	X	X
Canada	2.0	1.7

COUNTRIES	1970–1975	1990–1995
Costa Rica	4.3	3.0
Cuba	3.6	1.9
Dominican Republic	5.6	3.3
El Salvador	6.1	4.5
Guatemala	6.5	5.4
Haiti	5.8	4.8
Honduras	7.4	4.9
Jamaica	5.0	2.4
Mexico	6.4	3.1
Nicaragua	6.7	5.0
Panama	4.9	2.9
Trinidad and Tobago	3.5	2.7
United States	2.0	1.9
SOUTH AMERICA	**4.6**	**3.2**
Argentina	3.2	2.8
Bolivia	6.5	5.8
Brazil	4.7	3.2
Chile	3.6	2.7
Colombia	4.7	2.9
Ecuador	6.1	3.9
Guyana	4.9	2.4
Paraguay	5.7	4.3
Peru	6.0	3.6
Suriname	5.3	2.6
Uruguay	3.0	2.3
Venezuela	5.0	3.5
ASIA	**5.1**	**3.3**
Afghanistan	7.1	6.8
Bahrain	5.9	3.7
Bangladesh	7.0	5.1
Bhutan	5.7	5.5
Cambodia	5.5	4.4
China	4.8	2.3
Cyprus	2.2	2.2
India	5.4	4.1
Indonesia	5.1	3.1
Iran	6.5	4.7
Iraq	7.1	5.9
Israel	3.8	2.8
Japan	2.1	1.7
Jordan	7.8	5.5
Korea, North	5.7	2.4
Korea, South	4.1	1.7
Kuwait	6.9	3.5
Laos	6.2	6.7
Lebanon	4.9	3.4
Malaysia	5.2	3.5
Mongolia	5.8	4.7
Myanmar (Burma)	5.4	3.7
Nepal	6.5	5.5
Oman	7.2	7.1
Pakistan	7.0	5.9
Philippines	5.3	3.9
Qatar	6.8	5.3
Saudi Arabia	7.3	7.1
Singapore	2.6	1.8
Sri Lanka	4.0	2.5
Syria	7.7	6.3
Thailand	5.0	2.2
Turkey	5.0	3.3
United Arab Emirates	6.4	4.3
Vietnam	5.9	3.7
Yemen	8.0	7.6

(continued on next page)

COUNTRIES	1970–1975	1990–1995	COUNTRIES	1970–1975	1990–1995
EUROPE	**2.2**	**1.7**	Norway	2.3	1.7
Albania	4.7	2.7	Poland	2.3	2.1
Austria	2.0	1.5	Portugal	2.8	1.7
Belgium	1.9	1.7	Romania	2.6	2.0
Bulgaria	2.2	1.8	Spain	2.9	1.7
Czechoslovakia[2]	2.3	2.0	Sweden	1.9	1.9
Denmark	2.0	1.5	Switzerland	1.8	1.6
Finland	1.6	1.7	United Kingdom	2.0	1.8
France	2.3	1.8	U.S.S.R.[3]	2.4	2.3
Germany	1.6	1.4	Yugoslavia[4]	2.3	1.9
Greece	2.3	1.7			
Hungary	2.1	1.8	**OCEANIA**	**3.2**	**2.4**
Iceland	2.8	1.9	Australia	2/5	1.8
Ireland	3.8	2.4	Fiji	3.7	2.8
Italy	2.3	1.4	New Zealand	2.8	2.0
Luxembourg	2.0	1.5	Papua New Guinea	6.1	4.8
Malta	2.1	1.9	Solomon Islands	X	X
Netherlands	2.0	1.6			

[1]Total fertility rate is an estimate of the number of children that an average woman would have if current age-specific fertility rates remained constant during her reproductive years.

[2]On January 1, 1993, Czechoslovakia was separated by peaceful agreement into two independent countries, the Czech Republic and the Slovak Republic. At the time of this printing, information was not yet available for these two separate countries.

[3]At the time of this printing, separate statistical data on the countries of the Commonwealth of Independent States were not yet available, nor were there available data on the former Soviet republics that are not members of the C.I.S. The data for the former U.S.S.R. thus include information for Russia and the other Commonwealth countries of Armenia, Azerbaijan, Belarus, Kazakhstan, Kyrgyzstan, Moldova, Tajikistan, Turkmenistan, Ukraine, and Uzbekistan, along with the non-Commonwealth countries of Estonia, Georgia, Latvia, and Lithuania.

[4]At the time of this printing, separate statistical data on the countries that made up the former state of Yugoslavia were not yet available. The data for Yugoslavia thus include information for the Federal Republic of Yugoslavia (Serbia and Montenegro) and the independent countries of Bosnia-Herzegovina, Croatia, Macedonia, and Slovenia.

Sources: United Nations Population Division; *World Resources 1992–93.*

Table F

World Countries: Literacy Rates, 1970–1990

COUNTRIES	ADULT FEMALE 1970 (%)	ADULT FEMALE 1990 (%)	ADULT MALE 1970 (%)	ADULT MALE 1990 (%)
AFRICA				
Algeria	11	46	39	70
Angola	7	29	16	56
Benin	8	16	23	32
Botswana	44	65	37	84
Burkina Faso	3	9	13	28
Burundi	10	40	29	61
Cameroon	19	43	47	66
Cape Verde	X	X	X	X
Central African Republic	6	25	26	52
Chad	2	18	20	42
Comoros	X	X	X	X
Congo	19	44	50	70
Djibouti	X	X	X	X
Egypt	20	34	50	63
Equatorial Guinea	X	37	X	64
Ethiopia	X	X	8	X
Gabon	22	49	43	74
Gambia	X	16	X	39
Ghana	18	51	43	70
Guinea	7	13	21	35
Guinea-Bissau	6	24	13	50
Ivory Coast	10	40	26	67
Kenya	19	59	44	80
Lesotho	74	X	49	X
Liberia	8	29	27	50
Libya	13	50	60	75
Madagascar	43	73	56	88
Malawi	18	X	42	X
Mali	4	24	11	41
Mauritania	X	21	X	47
Mauritius	59	X	77	X
Morocco	10	38	34	61
Mozambique	14	21	29	45
Namibia	X	X	X	X
Niger	2	17	6	40
Nigeria	14	40	35	62
Rwanda	21	37	43	64
Senegal	5	25	18	52
Sierra Leone	8	11	5	31
Somalia	1	14	5	36
South Africa	X	X	X	X
Sudan	6	12	28	43
Swaziland	X	X	X	X
Tanzania	18	X	48	X
Togo	7	31	27	56
Tunisia	17	56	44	74
Uganda	30	35	52	62
Zaire	22	61	61	84
Zambia	37	65	66	81
Zimbabwe	47	60	63	74
NORTH AND CENTRAL AMERICA				
Barbados	X	X	X	X
Belize	X	X	X	X
Canada	X	X	X	X
Costa Rica	87	93	88	93
Cuba	87	93	86	95
Dominican Republic	65	82	69	85
El Salvador	53	70	61	76

COUNTRIES	ADULT FEMALE 1970 (%)	ADULT FEMALE 1990 (%)	ADULT MALE 1970 (%)	ADULT MALE 1990 (%)
Guatemala	37	47	51	63
Haiti	17	47	26	59
Honduras	50	71	55	76
Jamaica	97	99	96	98
Mexico	69	95	78	90
Nicaragua	57	X	58	X
Panama	81	88	81	88
Trinidad and Tobago	X	X	X	X
United States	99	X	99	X
SOUTH AMERICA				
Argentina	92	95	94	96
Bolivia	46	71	68	85
Brazil	63	80	69	85
Chile	88	93	90	94
Colombia	76	86	79	88
Ecuador	68	84	75	88
Guyana	89	95	94	98
Paraguay	75	88	85	92
Peru	60	79	81	92
Suriname	X	95	X	95
Uruguay	93	96	93	97
Venezuela	71	90	79	87
ASIA				
Afghanistan	2	14	13	44
Bahrain	X	69	X	82
Bangladesh	12	22	36	47
Bhutan	X	25	X	51
Cambodia	23	22	X	48
China	X	62	X	84
Cyprus	X	X	X	X
India	20	34	47	62
Indonesia	42	68	66	84
Iran	17	43	40	65
Iraq	18	49	50	70
Israel	83	X	93	X
Japan	99	X	99	X
Jordan	29	70	64	89
Korea, North	X	X	X	X
Korea, South	81	94	94	99
Kuwait	42	67	65	77
Laos	28	X	37	X
Lebanon	58	73	79	88
Malaysia	48	70	71	87
Mongolia	74	X	87	X
Myanmar	57	72	85	89
Nepal	3	13	23	38
Oman	X	X	X	X
Pakistan	11	21	30	47
Philippines	81	90	84	90
Qatar	X	X	X	X
Saudi Arabia	2	48	15	73
Singapore	55	X	82	X
Sri Lanka	69	84	85	93
Syria	20	51	60	78
Thailand	72	90	86	96
Turkey	34	71	69	90
United Arab Emirates	7	X	24	X
Vietnam	X	84	X	92
Yemen	4	26	20	53
EUROPE				
Albania	X	X	X	X
Austria	X	X	X	X

(continued on next page)

COUNTRIES	ADULT FEMALE 1970 (%)	ADULT FEMALE 1990 (%)	ADULT MALE 1970 (%)	ADULT MALE 1990 (%)
Belgium	99	X	99	X
Bulgaria	89	X	94	X
Czechoslovakia[1]	X	X	X	X
Denmark	X	X	X	X
Finland	X	X	X	X
France	98	X	99	X
Germany	X	X	X	X
Greece	76	89	93	98
Hungary	98	X	98	X
Iceland	X	X	X	X
Ireland	X	X	X	X
Italy	93	96	95	98
Luxembourg	X	X	X	X
Malta	X	X	X	X
Netherlands	X	X	X	X
Norway	X	X	X	X
Poland	97	X	98	X
Portugal	65	82	78	89
Romania	91	X	96	X
Spain	87	93	93	97
Sweden	X	X	X	X
Switzerland	X	X	X	X
United Kingdom	X	X	X	X
U.S.S.R.[2]	97	X	98	X
Yugoslavia[3]	76	88	92	97
OCEANIA				
Australia	X	X	X	X
Fiji	X	X	X	X
New Zealand	X	X	X	X
Papua New Guinea	24	38	39	65
Solomon Islands	X	X	X	X

[1]On January 1, 1993, Czechoslovakia was separated by peaceful agreement into two independent countries, the Czech Republic and the Slovak Republic. At the time of this printing, information was not yet available for these two separate countries.

[2]At the time of this printing, separate statistical data on the countries of the Commonwealth of Independent States were not yet available, nor were there available data on the former Soviet republics that are not members of the C.I.S. The data for the former U.S.S.R. thus include information for Russia and the other Commonwealth countries of Armenia, Azerbaijan, Belarus, Kazakhstan, Kyrgyzstan, Moldova, Tajikistan, Turkmenistan, Ukraine, and Uzbekistan, along with the non-Commonwealth countries of Estonia, Georgia, Latvia, and Lithuania.

[3]At the time of this printing, separate statistical data on the countries that made up the former state of Yugoslavia were not yet available. The data for Yugoslavia thus include information for the Federal Republic of Yugoslavia (Serbia and Montenegro) and the independent countries of Bosnia-Herzegovina, Croatia, Macedonia, and Slovenia.

Sources: United Nations Childrens' Fund; United Nations Development Programme; UNESCO; World Resources 1992–93.

Part V

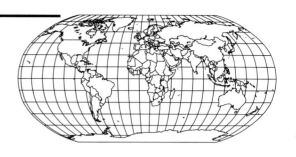

Food and Agriculture

Map 26 Production of Staple Food Crops

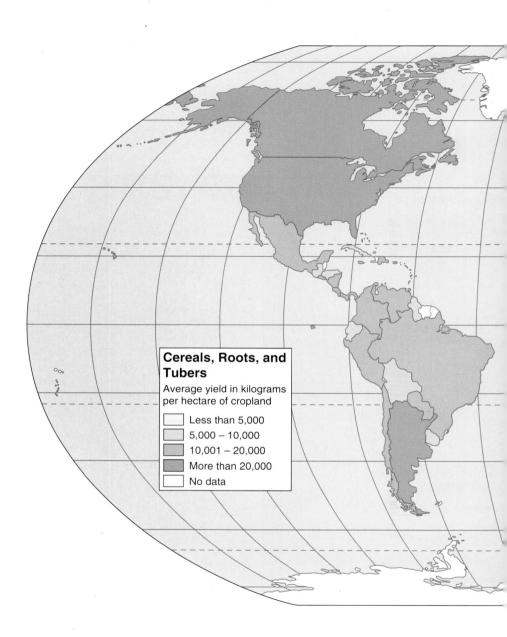

Cereals, Roots, and Tubers

Average yield in kilograms per hectare of cropland

- [ ] Less than 5,000
- [ ] 5,000 – 10,000
- [ ] 10,001 – 20,000
- [ ] More than 20,000
- [ ] No data

For most of the world's population, the production of crops (as opposed to livestock foods) provides the bulk of dietary intake. Global production of the staple (most important) food crops has increased over the last 10 years—but so has global population. In Africa, for example, despite a 30 percent increase in staple crop production since 1981, per capita food output has dropped more than 5 percent because of a population growth that is faster than the growth in agricultural output. The map illustrates considerable regional differences in outputs of food staples per areal unit of cropland. On a global average, 1 hectare (2.47 acres) of cropland in 1990 yielded about 2.6 metric tons (2,600 kilograms) of cereals or about 11.8 metric tons of roots and tubers. Yet in

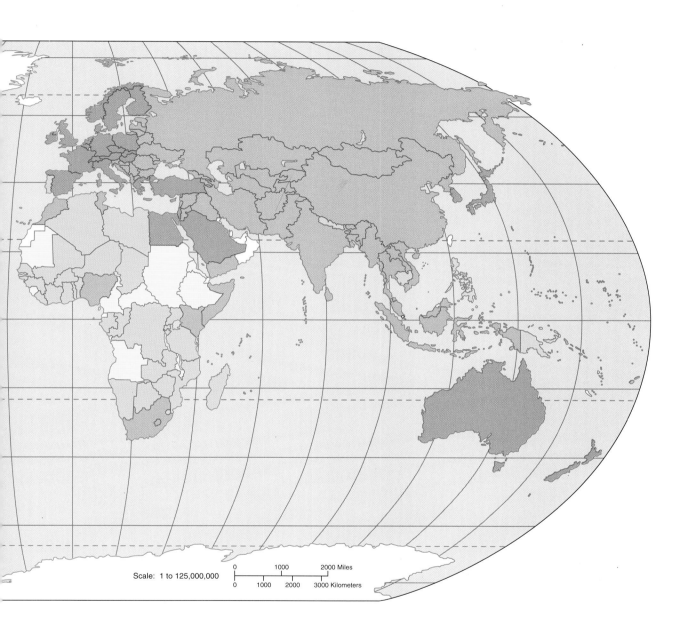

Scale: 1 to 125,000,000

0   1000   2000 Miles

0   1000   2000   3000 Kilometers

Africa, 1 hectare yielded only 1.2 metric tons of cereals or 7.9 metric tons of roots and tubers. In Europe, on the other hand, 1 hectare yielded 4.2 and 21.2 metric tons of cereals or roots and tubers respectively. Such great differences are explainable primarily in terms of agricultural inputs: different farming methods, varying levels of fertilizers, agricultural chemicals, irrigation, and machinery. The European farmer applies 2.3 times more fertilizer per hectare than the global average; the African farmer only one-fifth of the global average. These conditions are not likely to change and the map may be viewed not just as an indicator of present agricultural output but of potential food production as well.

Map 27 Agricultural Production Per Capita

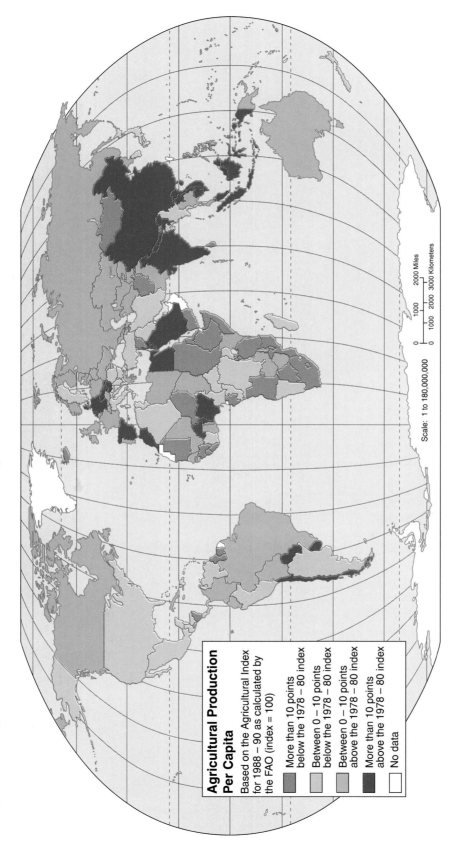

Agricultural Production Per Capita

Based on the Agricultural Index for 1988 – 90 as calculated by the FAO (index = 100)

- More than 10 points below the 1978 – 80 index
- Between 0 – 10 points below the 1978 – 80 index
- Between 0 – 10 points above the 1978 – 80 index
- More than 10 points above the 1978 – 80 index
- No data

Scale: 1 to 180,000,000

0   1000   2000 Miles
0   1000 2000 3000 Kilometers

Agricultural production includes the value of all crop and livestock products originating within a country for the base period of 1988–1990. The index value portrays the disposable output (after deductions for livestock feed and seed for planting) of a country's agriculture in comparison with the base period 1978–1980. Thus, the production values show not only the relative ability of countries to produce food but also show whether or not that ability has increased or decreased over the 10-year period from 1978–1980 to 1988–1990. In general, agricultural production in Africa and in Central America has fallen while production in South America, Asia, and Europe has risen. In the case of Africa, the drop in production reflects a population growing more rapidly than agricultural productivity. Where rapid increases in food production

per capita exist (such as in certain countries in South America, Asia, and Europe), most often the reason is the development of new agricultural technologies that allowed food production to grow faster than population. In much of Asia, for example, the so-called "Green Revolution" of new highly productive strains of wheat and rice made possible positive index values. Also in Asia, the cessation of major warfare allowed some countries (Cambodia, Laos, Vietnam) to show substantial increases over the 1978–1980 index. In some cases, a drop in production per capita reflects government decisions to limit production in order to maintain higher prices for agricultural products. The United States and Japan fall into this category. This map should be compared with the following map to get a full picture of countries' abilities to feed themselves.

Map 28 Global Nutrition

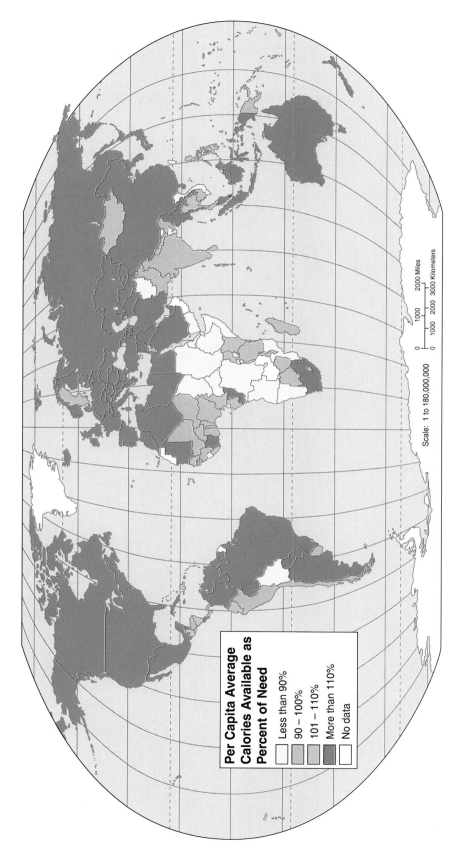

**Per Capita Average
Calories Available as
Percent of Need**

- Less than 90%
- 90 – 100%
- 101 – 110%
- More than 110%
- No data

Scale: 1 to 180,000,000

0   1000   2000 Miles

0 1000 2000 3000 Kilometers

The data shown on this map indicates the presence or absence of critical food shortages. While they do not necessarily indicate the presence of starvation or famine, they certainly do indicate potential problem areas for the next decade. The measurements are in calories from *all* food sources: domestic production, international trade, drawdown on stocks or food reserves, and direct foreign contributions or aid. The quantity of calories available is that amount, estimated by the UN's Food and Agricultural Organization (FAO), that actually reaches consumers. The calories actually consumed may be lower than the figures shown, depending on how much is lost in a variety of ways: home storage (loss to pests such as rats and mice), loss in preparation and cooking, consumption by pets and domestic animals, discarded foods, and so on. The estimate of need is not a global uniform value but is calculated for each country on the basis of the age and sex distribution of the population and the estimated level of activity of the population. Compare this map with the one immediately before it for a good measure of potential problem areas for food shortages within the next decade.

Table G
World Countries: Agricultural Operations, 1989

NOTES: kg = kilogram; 1 kilogram = 2.205 lbs.
ha = hectare; 1 hectare = 2.471 acres

COUNTRIES	CROPLAND (thousands of hectares)	IRRIGATED LAND (% of cropland)	FERTILIZER USE (kg/ha cropland)	PESTICIDE USE (kg/ha cropland)	TRACTORS AVERAGE NUMBER	TRACTORS % CHANGE 1979–1989
WORLD	1,478,190	16	97	X[1]	25,895,523	26
AFRICA	186,995	6	20	X	569,554	30
Algeria	7,605	4	27	21,400	93,757	116
Angola	3,600	X	5	X	10,270	3
Benin	1,860	0	3	X	123	26
Botswana	1,380	0	1	X	4,217	111
Burkina Faso	3,564	0	5	X	125	23
Burundi	1,336	5	3	59	129	110
Cameroon	7,008	0	6	X	1,003	147
Cape Verde	39	5	0	X	16	37
Central African Republic	2,006	X	0	X	195	38
Chad	3,205	0	2	X	165	10
Comoros	100	X	0	X	X	X
Congo	168	2	8	X	695	5
Djibouti	X	X	X	X	8	33
Egypt	2,585	99	384	19,567	52,497	85
Equatorial Guinea	230	X	0	X	100	3
Ethiopia	13,930	1	6	993	3,900	2
Gabon	452	X	3	X	1,427	24
Gambia	178	7	17	101	43	-7
Ghana	2,720	0	4	X	3,900	16
Guinea	728	3	1	X	250	108
Guinea-Bissau	335	X	1	X	48	11
Ivory Coast	3,660	2	10	X	3,450	21
Kenya	2,428	2	47	1,307	9,538	51
Lesotho	320	X	15	X	1,750	37
Liberia	373	1	10	310	324	16
Libya	2,150	11	40	2,017	31,367	61
Madagascar	3,092	29	3	1,630	2,847	12
Malawi	2,409	1	21	X	1,380	25
Mali	2,093	10	6	683	835	3
Mauritania	199	6	10	X	322	29
Mauritius	106	16	302	961	350	11
Morocco	9,241	14	34	3,350	34.067	42
Mozambique	3,100	4	1	X	5,750	2
Namibia	662	1	X	X	2,950	20
Niger	3,605	1	1	159	179	31
Nigeria	31,335	3	10	4,000	11,033	36
Rwanda	1,153	0	1	X	88	8
Senegal	5,226	3	5	X	477	13
Sierra Leone	1,801	2	0	X	510	320
Somalia	1,039	11	3	X	2,100	39
South Africa	13,174	9	58	11,053	183,233	2
Sudan	12,510	15	4	X	21,000	106
Swaziland	164	38	47	X	3,293	15
Tanzania	5,250	3	9	5,733	18,550	1
Togo	1,444	0	8	X	353	126
Tunisia	4,700	6	22	1,330	25,967	3
Uganda	6,705	0	0	23	4,200	89
Zaire	7,850	0	1	X	2,333	37
Zambia	5,268	1	17	X	5,709	30
Zimbabwe	2,810	8	56	207	20,367	3

(continued on next page)

COUNTRIES	CROPLAND (thousands of hectares)	IRRIGATED LAND (% of cropland)	FERTILIZER USE (kg/ha cropland)	PESTICIDE USE (kg/ha cropland)	TRACTORS AVERAGE NUMBER	TRACTORS % CHANGE 1979–1989
NORTH AND CENTRAL AMERICA	**273,634**	**9**	**85**	**X**	**5,709,463**	**-2**
Barbados	33	X	91	X	608	15
Belize	56	4	71	X	1,050	39
Canada	45,960	2	47	54,767	756,300	16
Costa Rica	528	22	191	3,667	6,350	9
Cuba	3,329	26	192	9,567	75,368	12
Dominican Republic	1,446	16	50	3,297	2,307	9
El Salvador	733	16	121	2,838	3,407	8
Guatemala	1,875	4	69	5,117	4,160	7
Haiti	905	8	3	X	215	30
Honduras	1,810	5	20	859	3,420	11
Jamaica	269	13	105	1,420	3,037	12
Mexico	24,710	21	73	27,630	165,333	53
Nicaragua	1,273	7	55	2,003	2,510	34
Panama	577	5	62	2,393	6,230	29
Trinidad and Tobago	120	18	28	X	2,620	16
United States	189,915	10	95	373,333	4,670,000	-6
SOUTH AMERICA	**142,134**	**6**	**40**	**X**	**1,089,234**	**43**
Argentina	35,750	5	5	14,313	209,333	20
Bolivia	3,460	5	2	833	4,690	30
Brazil	78,650	3	46	46,698	680,000	59
Chile	4,525	28	73	1,800	38,447	12
Colombia	5,380	9	90	16,100	34,711	31
Ecuador	2,653	21	30	3,110	8,400	49
Guyana	495	26	29	658	3,580	5
Paraguay	2,216	3	6	3,423	10,500	107
Peru	3,730	33	54	2,753	16,000	26
Suriname	68	85	74	1,720	1,250	17
Uruguay	1,304	8	48	1,517	35,200	9
Venezuela	3,895	7	162	8,143	46,833	33
ASIA	**454,115**	**32**	**111**	**X**	**5,122,884**	**87**
Afghanistan	8,054	33	8	605	770	3
Bahrain	2	50	333	X	X	X
Bangladesh	9,292	26	86	234	5,083	39
Bhutan	131	26	0	X	X	X
Cambodia	3,056	3	0	833	1,363	1
China	96,115	47	255	159,267	878,453	54
Cyprus	156	21	141	X	13,583	30
India	168,990	25	62	53,087	791,289	136
Indonesia	21,260	35	113	16,344	16,100	75
Iran	14,830	39	72	X	112,667	77
Iraq	5,450	42	39	X	39,062	95
Israel	433	49	234	847	28,502	18
Japan	4,637	62	425	32,000	1,979,260	89
Jordan	376	15	63	X	5,682	35
Korea, North	2,000	68	396	X	71,000	116
Korea, South	2,127	64	411	12,273	25,269	1,494
Kuwait	4	50	167	X	117	343
Laos	901	13	0	X	840	92
Lebanon	301	29	79	X	3,000	0
Malaysia	4,880	7	150	9,730	11,833	57
Mongolia	1,375	5	15	X	11,681	23
Myanmar	10,034	10	11	15,300	10,872	30
Nepal	2,641	34	23	X	2,870	50
Oman	48	85	83	X	136	54
Pakistan	20,730	78	85	1,856	176,000	136
Philippines	7,970	20	64	4,415	8,077	-25
Qatar	5	X	200	X	90	79

(continued on next page)

COUNTRIES	CROPLAND (thousands of hectares)	IRRIGATED LAND (% of cropland)	FERTILIZER USE (kg/ha cropland)	PESTICIDE USE (kg/ha cropland)	AVERAGE NUMBER	% CHANGE 1979–1989
Saudi Arabia	1,185	36	398	X	1,850	85
Singapore	1	X	6,000	X	59	49
Sri Lanka	1,901	29	107	697	29,000	54
Syria	5,503	12	46	4,892	54,767	137
Thailand	22,126	19	33	22,289	142,667	206
Turkey	27,885	8	62	9,000	654,336	80
United Arab Emirates	39	13	120	X	X	X
Vietnam	6,600	28	79	883	35,533	30
Yemen	1,481	23	7	325	5,034	31
EUROPE	**139,865**	**12**	**227**	**X**	**10,244,872**	**30**
Albania	707	59	141	5,183	11,443	14
Austria	1,553	0	210	4,548	339,168	8
Belgium	822	0	505	13,263	121,896	10
Bulgaria	4,146	30	199	32,400	53,510	-17
Czechoslovakia[2]	5,108	6	313	14,970	140,494	1
Denmark	2,555	17	243	7,729	166,210	-13
Finland	2,453	3	205	2,639	242,667	21
France	19,119	6	312	98,733	1,511,711	7
Germany	12,391	4	387	24,115	1,615,437	-15
Greece	3,924	30	165	29,240	187,000	53
Hungary	5,287	3	258	27,595	52,200	-10
Iceland	8	X	2,792	5	13,067	6
Ireland	953	X	717	2,250	163,667	26
Italy	12,033	26	172	98,496	1,362,786	43
Luxembourg	X	X	X	X	X	X
Malta	13	8	77	X	448	11
Netherlands	934	58	662	9,670	194,000	15
Norway	878	11	252	1,508	153,491	27
Poland	14,759	1	224	15,277	1,099,139	111
Portugal	3,771	17	75	16,016	77,173	25
Romania	10,350	33	135	17,237	166,883	20
Spain	20,345	16	101	71,553	700,869	54
Sweden	2,853	4	134	5,736	183,000	-2
Switzerland	412	6	430	1,699	109,000	25
United Kingdom	6,736	2	359	34,147	518,165	6
U.S.S.R.[3]	230,630	9	114	535,400	2,742,667	11
Yugoslavia[4]	7,766	2	126	31,567	1,061,000	211
OCEANIA	**50,617**	**4**	**33**	**X**	**417,858**	**-2**
Australia	48,934	4	26	65,200	332,000	0
Fiji	240	0	97	X	4,290	13
New Zealand	507	54	670	1,793	78,433	-11
Papua New Guinea	388	X	39	X	1,150	-7
Solomon Islands	57	X	X	X	X	X

[1]In this table "X" indicates "No Data" as it does in all other tables in the Atlas. However, in most instances, the "X" indicates that there are no measurable uses of pesticides. Even where individual farmers in some nations may use pesticides, their applications are in amounts well below 100 metric tons.

[2]On January 1, 1993, Czechoslovakia was separated by peaceful agreement into two independent countries, the Czech Republic and the Slovak Republic. At the time of this printing, information was not yet available for these two separate countries.

[3]At the time of this printing, separate statistical data on the countries of the Commonwealth of Independent States were not yet available, nor were there available data on the former Soviet republics that are not members of the C.I.S. The data for the former U.S.S.R. thus include information for Russia and the other Commonwealth countries of Armenia, Azerbaijan, Belarus, Kazakhstan, Kyrgyzstan, Moldova, Tajikistan, Turkmenistan, Ukraine, and Uzbekistan, along with the non-Commonwealth countries of Estonia, Georgia, Latvia, and Lithuania.

[4]At the time of this printing, separate statistical data on the countries that made up the former state of Yugoslavia were not yet available. The data for Yugoslavia thus include information for the Federal Republic of Yugoslavia (Serbia and Montenegro) and the independent countries of Bosnia-Herzegovina, Croatia, Macedonia, and Slovenia.

Sources: Food and Agriculture Organization of the United Nations; United Nations Industrial Development Organization; *World Resources 1992–93.*

Part VI

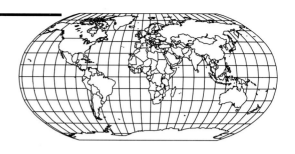

Energy and Materials

Map 29 World Energy Resources

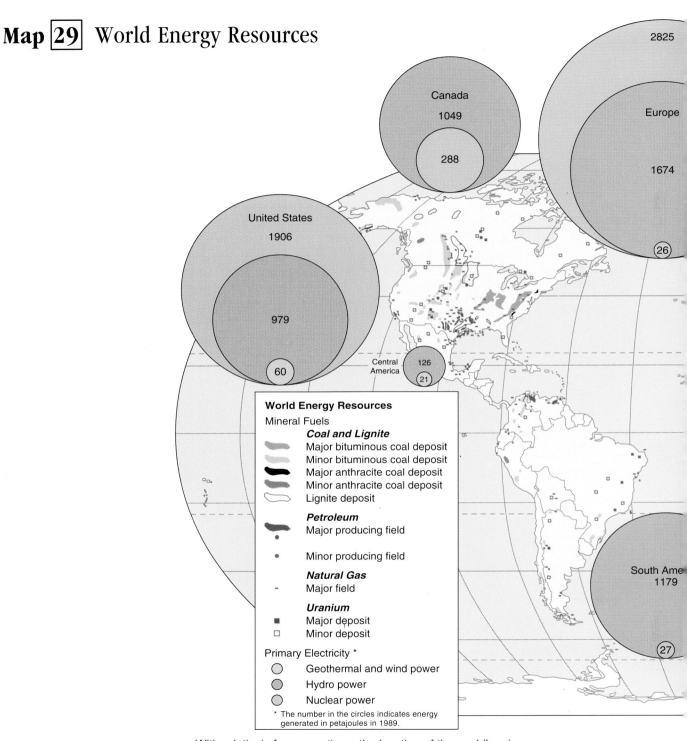

Canada
1049
288
2825

Europe
1674
26

United States
1906
979
60

Central America
126
21

South America
1179
27

World Energy Resources

Mineral Fuels

Coal and Lignite
Major bituminous coal deposit
Minor bituminous coal deposit
Major anthracite coal deposit
Minor anthracite coal deposit
Lignite deposit

Petroleum
Major producing field

Minor producing field

Natural Gas
Major field

Uranium
Major deposit
Minor deposit

Primary Electricity *
Geothermal and wind power
Hydro power
Nuclear power

* The number in the circles indicates energy generated in petajoules in 1989.

With relatively few exceptions, the location of the world's primary energy sources coincides with regions of high economic development. Countries such as the United States, Canada, and Russia contain enormous reserves of oil, natural gas, coal, and uranium, and also possess vast potential for the development of alternative energy such as geothermal power, wind power, solar power, and hydroelectric power (all primary generators of electricity). Central and South America are limited in their energy resources, except for the oil fields of Mexico and Venezuela (which supply the needs of the United States). Africa is largely devoid of energy resources, with the exception

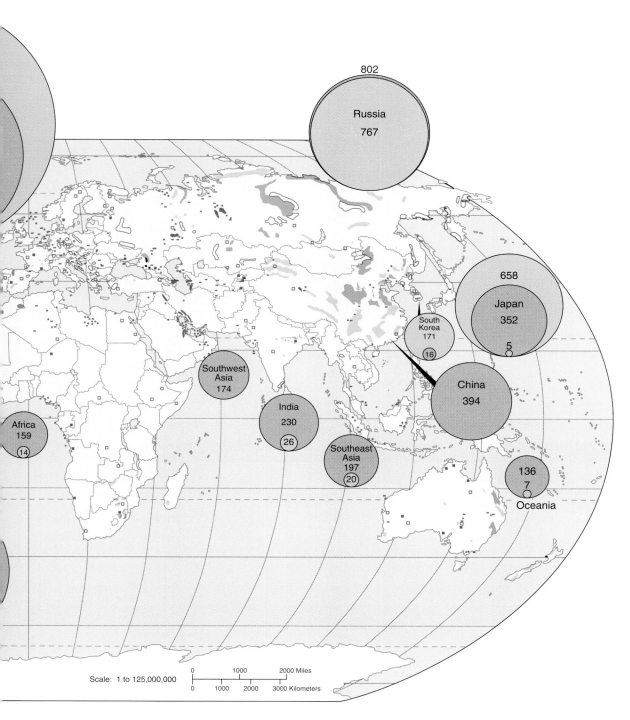

of scattered oil deposits in the North and West African states. Asia has abundant oil, but it is concentrated largely in the huge oil fields of the Persian Gulf states, the scattered oil reserves of Indonesia, and in the coal deposits of India and China. While some uranium deposits exist in South America and Africa, they are costly to work and the technology is not affordable for the conversion of uranium to electricity through nuclear power generator stations. As much as any other factor of physical geography, the location of energy resources separates the "haves" from the "have nots."

Map 30 Energy Production Per Capita

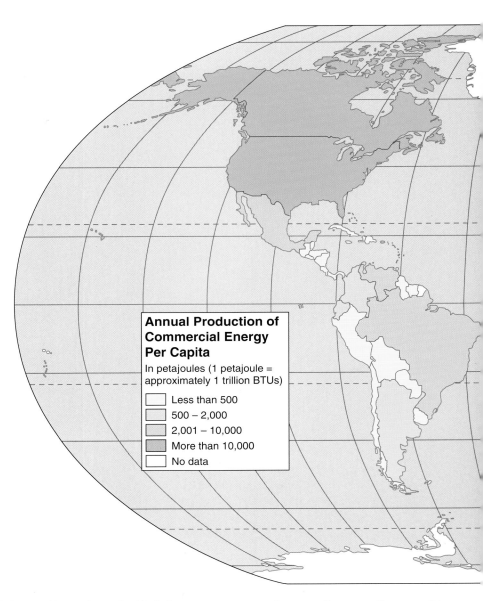

Annual Production of Commercial Energy Per Capita

In petajoules (1 petajoule = approximately 1 trillion BTUs)

- Less than 500
- 500 – 2,000
- 2,001 – 10,000
- More than 10,000
- No data

It is one thing to have the kind of energy resources shown on the preceding map; it is another thing to turn those resources into energy. The production of commercial energy in all its forms—solid fuels (primarily coal), liquid fuels (primarily petroleum), natural gas, geothermal, wind, solar, hydroelectric, nuclear—is a good measure of economic potential, indicating the ability to produce sufficient quantities of energy either to meet domestic demands or to provide a healthy export commodity—or, in some instances, both. Commercial energy production is also a measure of the level of economic development—although a fairly subjective one. In general, the wealthier countries produce more energy from all sources (partly because they use more) than do the poorer countries. This general relationship has its exceptions, however. Countries such as Japan and many of the European nations rank among the world's

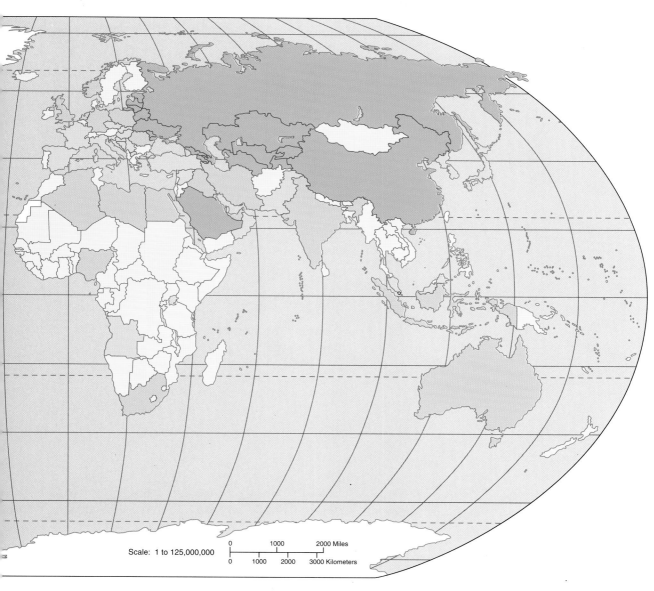

Scale: 1 to 125,000,000

0 1000 2000 Miles

0 1000 2000 3000 Kilometers

wealthiest, but are energy-poor and produce very little of their own energy. They have the ability, however, to pay for it. On the other hand, countries such as those of the Persian Gulf or the oil-producing countries of Latin America may rank relatively low on the scale of economic development but rank high as producers of energy. The map does not show the enormous amounts of energy from noncommercial sources used by the world's poor, particularly in Latin America, South Asia, and East Asia. In the developing countries, firewood and animal dung may account for more actual energy production than coal or oil. Indeed, for many in the Third World, the real energy crisis is a shortage of wood for cooking and heating. You may be able to judge the variations between the production and use of commercial and noncommercial energy by comparing this map with the following one on energy consumption.

Map 31 Energy Requirements Per Capita

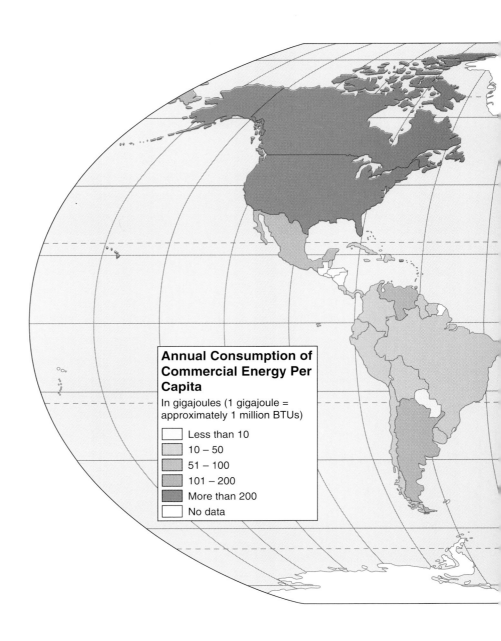

Annual Consumption of Commercial Energy Per Capita

In gigajoules (1 gigajoule = approximately 1 million BTUs)

- Less than 10
- 10 – 50
- 51 – 100
- 101 – 200
- More than 200
- No data

Of all the quantitative measures of economic well-being, energy consumption per capita may be the most expressive. Of the world's 25 countries defined as having high incomes, all consume at least 100 gigajoules of commercial energy (the equivalent of about 3½ metric tons of coal) per person per year, with some, such as the United States and Canada, having consumption rates in the 300 gigajoule range (the equivalent of more than 10 metric tons of coal per person per year). With the exception of the oil-rich Persian Gulf states, where consumption figures include the costly "burning off"

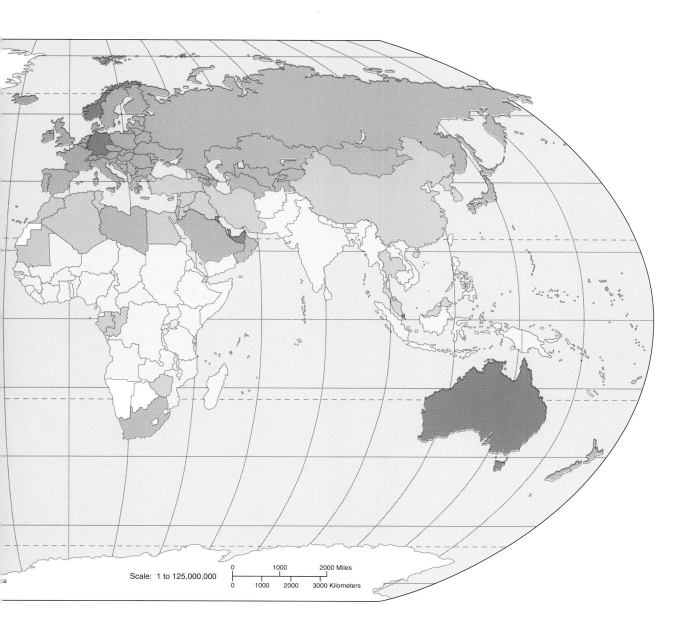

Scale: 1 to 125,000,000

0   1000   2000 Miles

0   1000   2000   3000 Kilometers

of excess energy in the form of natural gas, most of the highest consumer countries are in the Northern Hemisphere, concentrated in North America and Western Europe. At the other end of the scale are those countries defined as low-income economies where consumption rates are often less than 1 percent those of the United States and other high consumers. These figures do not, of course, include the consumption of noncommercial energy—firewood, animal dung, dried grasses, and other organic matter—widely used in the lesser-developed parts of the world.

Map 32 Production and Consumption of Selected Metals

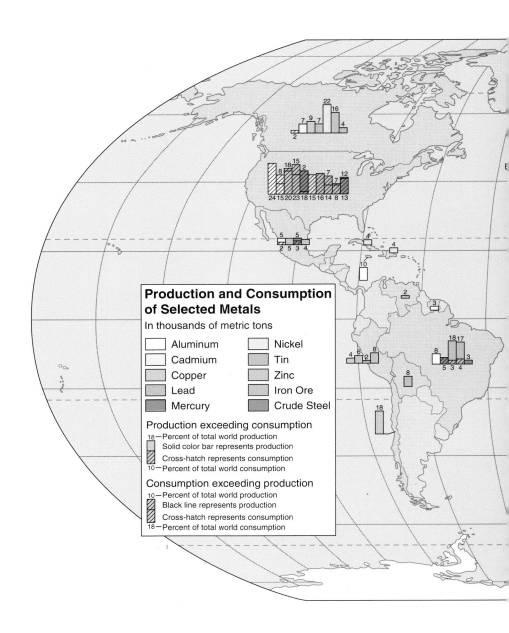

Production and Consumption of Selected Metals

In thousands of metric tons

Aluminum	Nickel
Cadmium	Tin
Copper	Zinc
Lead	Iron Ore
Mercury	Crude Steel

Production exceeding consumption

18—Percent of total world production
Solid color bar represents production
Cross-hatch represents consumption
10—Percent of total world consumption

Consumption exceeding production

10—Percent of total world production
Black line represents production
Cross-hatch represents consumption
18—Percent of total world consumption

The data on this map portray the top 10 producers and the top 10 consumers in 1990 of 10 selected metals. The bars of the graphs are proportional to the percentage of the total world production or consumption for each country. The annual production data include the metal content of the ore mined for copper, lead, mercury, nickel, tin, and zinc. Aluminum (or bauxite ore) and iron ore production are expressed in gross weight of ore mined. Cadmium production refers to the refined metal, and crude steel production refers to usable ingots, cast products, and liquid steel. Consumption data refer to the domestic use of refined metals (for example, the tons of steel used in the manufacture of automobiles). You will note that some of the world's top consumer nations of

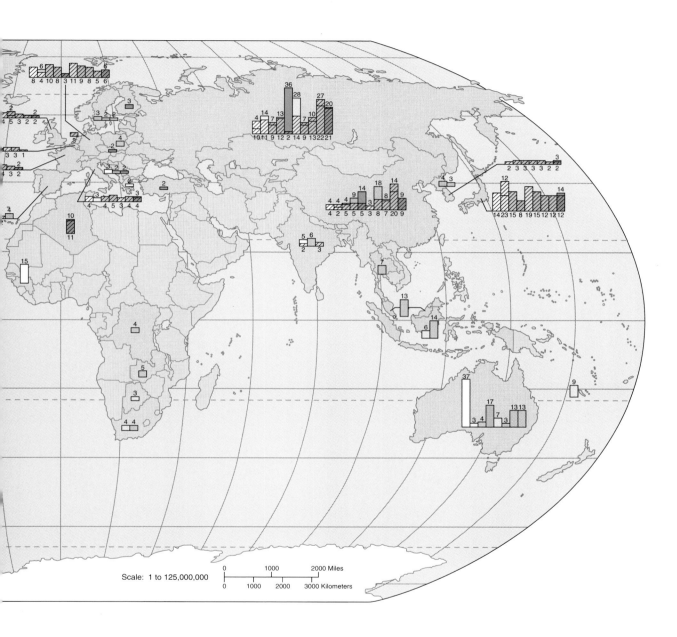

these critical metals are also among the world's top producer nations. The United States, for example, ranks in the top 4 consumers for each metal; but also ranks in the top 10 producer countries for 7 of the metals. Countries that rank among the top in both production and consumption are among the most highly developed nations. Countries that rank high as producers but not as consumers are often countries in a "colonial dependency" economy, producing raw materials for an export market and often at the mercy of the marketplace. Jamaica and Suriname, for example, depend extremely heavily upon the sale of bauxite ore (crude aluminum). When the United States, Japan, or Russia cut their use of aluminum, the economies of Jamaica and Suriname crash.

Table H

World Countries: Energy Production, Consumption, and Requirements, 1990

NOTES: 1 petajoule = 163,400 UN standard barrels of oil or 34,140 UN standard metric tons of coal.
Numbers in parentheses in imports column are net exporters of commercial energy.
Total consumption includes all sources, including noncommercial energy requirements.

	COMMERCIAL ENERGY			TOTAL ENERGY	
	COMMERCIAL PRODUCTION (petajoules)	COMMERCIAL CONSUMPTION (petajoules)	IMPORTS AS % OF CONSUMPTION (petajoules)	TOTAL CONSUMPTION (petajoules)	TRADITIONAL FUELS AS % TOTAL CONSUMPTION
WORLD	310,972	298	X	346,931	6
AFRICA	18,926	7,472	(153)	12,363	37
Algeria	3,869	666	(481)	666	3
Angola	959	25	(3,663)	78	55
Benin	12	6	(91)	54	86
Botswana	19	X	X	X	X
Burkina Faso	0	7	100	87	92
Burundi	1	3	79	43	92
Cameroon	345	85	(307)	204	49
Cape Verde	0	1	100	1	0
Central African Republic	0	4	93	38	88
Chad	0	3	99	36	92
Comoros	0	1	100	1	0
Congo	310	23	(1,249)	44	41
Djibouti	0	4	100	4	0
Egypt	2,142	1,122	(91)	1,211	4
Equatorial Guinea	0	1	100	6	75
Ethiopia	2	34	93	413	91
Gabon	462	42	(1,013)	71	35
Gambia	0	3	100	11	77
Ghana	17	46	63	236	67
Guinea	1	14	96	55	72
Guinea-Bissau	0	2	100	6	67
Ivory Coast	12	60	79	169	59
Kenya	10	72	86	434	79
Lesotho	X	X	X	X	X
Liberia	1	11	89	61	78
Libya	2,597	516	(404)	521	1
Madagascar	1	13	92	87	82
Malawi	2	10	79	146	90
Mali	1	6	90	59	87
Mauritania	0	41	100	42	0
Mauritius	0	14	97	30	52
Morocco	23	264	91	285	5
Mozambique	1	15	91	165	89
Namibia	0	X	X	X	X
Niger	5	13	65	55	73
Nigeria	3,747	592	(533)	1,589	62
Rwanda	1	6	89	62	88
Senegal	0	41	100	83	51
Sierra Leone	0	9	100	37	76
Somalia	0	12	100	81	85
South Africa	3,875	3,098	(25)	3,272	6
Sudan	2	45	96	254	81
Swaziland	6	X	X	X	X
Tanzania	2	28	92	339	90
Togo	0	7	100	16	43
Tunisia	224	167	(34)	197	15
Uganda	2	14	83	144	87
Zaire	77	65	(19)	422	76
Zambia	34	47	28	201	58
Zimbabwe	159	192	17	295	25

| | COMMERCIAL ENERGY | | | TOTAL ENERGY | |
	COMMERCIAL PRODUCTION (petajoules)	COMMERCIAL CONSUMPTION (petajoules)	IMPORTS AS % OF CONSUMPTION (petajoules)	TOTAL CONSUMPTION (petajoules)	TRADITIONAL FUELS AS % TOTAL CONSUMPTION
NORTH AND CENTRAL AMERICA	**78,990**	**87,638**	**10**	**98,570**	**2**
Barbados	3	12	72	14	12
Belize	0	3	100	6	55
Canada	10,830	8,414	(29)	11,087	1
Costa Rica	12	43	72	101	33
Cuba	32	471	93	650	27
Dominican Republic	3	81	96	115	23
El Salvador	7	34	80	87	46
Guatemala	15	52	71	156	57
Haiti	1	10	88	66	82
Honduras	3	26	88	89	62
Jamaica	0	61	99	67	8
Mexico	7,353	4,293	(71)	4,720	5
Nicaragua	2	31	93	71	49
Panama	8	41	81	76	26
Trinidad and Tobago	471	209	(125)	212	1
United States	60,249	73,370	18	80,560	2
SOUTH AMERICA	**12,610**	**8,803**	**(43)**	**14,240**	**20**
Argentina	1,905	1,813	(5)	2,070	5
Bolivia	165	79	(108)	105	16
Brazil	2,318	3,445	33	7,362	30
Chile	215	458	53	598	12
Colombia	1,657	775	(114)	1,119	17
Ecuador	663	200	(216)	308	24
Guyana	0	9	100	14	33
Paraguay	10	27	63	93	59
Peru	355	312	(14)	484	20
Suriname	13	15	18	22	2
Uruguay	14	71	80	119	24
Venezuela	5,325	1,592	(234)	1,860	1
ASIA	**85,244**	**70,778**	**(194)**	**84,136**	**10**
Afghanistan	123	107	(15)	157	29
Bahrain	292	228	(28)	228	0
Bangladesh	159	227	30	502	54
Bhutan	2	1	(189)	30	95
Cambodia	0	6	98	58	89
China	28,484	25,156	(9)	28,805	6
Cyprus	0	51	100	52	1
India	6,920	7,528	8	10,693	25
Indonesia	4,055	1,453	(180)	2,852	47
Iran	6,895	2,399	(187)	2,474	1
Iraq	5,993	567	(956)	572	0
Israel	2	402	99	399	0
Japan	1,381	14,533	90	16,573	0
Jordan	1	115	99	115	0
Korea, North	1,530	1,756	13	2,025	2
Korea, South	579	2,748	79	3,165	1
Kuwait	3,470	480	(624)	480	0
Laos	4	5	15	43	83
Lebanon	2	114	98	122	4
Malaysia	1,769	705	(151)	834	10
Mongolia	91	117	22	131	10
Myanmar	85	74	(15)	268	69
Nepal	2	13	85	226	92
Oman	1,435	146	(886)	146	0
Pakistan	600	930	36	1,330	21
Philippines	81	527	85	963	38

(continued on next page)

| | COMMERCIAL ENERGY | | | TOTAL ENERGY | |
	COMMERCIAL PRODUCTION (petajoules)	COMMERCIAL CONSUMPTION (petajoules)	IMPORTS AS % OF CONSUMPTION (petajoules)	TOTAL CONSUMPTION (petajoules)	TRADITIONAL FUELS AS % TOTAL CONSUMPTION
Qatar	1,076	250	(330)	250	0
Saudi Arabia	12,224	2,535	(382)	2,535	0
Singapore	0	393	100	393	0
Sri Lanka	10	55	83	153	52
Syria	793	340	(134)	374	0
Thailand	416	1,026	59	1,631	34
Turkey	642	1,539	58	1,766	5
United Arab Emirates	4,714	897	(425)	897	0
Vietnam	185	210	12	465	51
Yemen	353	112	(627)	116	1
EUROPE	**40,061**	**64,465**	**38**	**74,398**	**1**
Albania	185	119	(55)	156	10
Austria	250	892	72	1,153	1
Belgium	248	1,676	85	1,964	0
Bulgaria	528	1,291	59	1,381	1
Czechoslovakia[1]	1,871	2,733	32	2,975	1
Denmark	338	665	49	747	2
Finland	171	840	80	1,164	3
France	1,938	6,460	70	8,815	1
Germany	7,124	13,304	35	14,645	0
Greece	335	918	64	959	2
Hungary	608	1,136	46	1,344	2
Iceland	16	42	61	74	0
Ireland	139	392	65	400	0
Italy	938	6,384	85	6,942	1
Luxembourg	3	136	98	170	0
Malta	0	21	100	21	0
Netherlands	2,440	2,890	16	2,957	0
Norway	4,873	884	(451)	1,638	1
Poland	4,913	5,062	3	5,133	1
Portugal	25	543	95	598	1
Romania	2,308	3,047	24	3,228	1
Spain	854	2,846	70	3,399	1
Sweden	497	1,253	60	2,363	5
Switzerland	190	710	73	1,079	1
United Kingdom	8,211	8,436	3	9,047	0
U.S.S.R.[2]	69,071	54,958	(25)	58,599	1
Yugoslavia[3]	1,058	1,771	40	2,034	2
OCEANIA	**6,070**	**4,141**	**(25)**	**4,624**	**4**
Australia	5,656	3,534	(60)	3,770	3
Fiji	1	11	89	25	48
New Zealand	409	499	18	666	0
Papua New Guinea	2	33	95	91	60
Solomon Islands	0	2	100	4	38

[1]On January 1, 1993, Czechoslovakia was separated by peaceful agreement into two independent countries, the Czech Republic and the Slovak Republic. At the time of this printing, information was not yet available for these two separate countries.

[2]At the time of this printing, separate statistical data on the countries of the Commonwealth of Independent States were not yet available, nor were there available data on the former Soviet republics that are not members of the C.I.S. The data for the former U.S.S.R. thus include information for Russia and the other Commonwealth countries of Armenia, Azerbaijan, Belarus, Kazakhstan, Kyrgyzstan, Moldova, Tajikistan, Turkmenistan, Ukraine, and Uzbekistan, along with the non-Commonwealth countries of Estonia, Georgia, Latvia, and Lithuania.

[3]At the time of this printing, separate statistical data on the countries that made up the former state of Yugoslavia were not yet available. The data for Yugoslavia thus include information for the Federal Republic of Yugoslavia (Serbia and Montenegro) and the independent countries of Bosnia-Herzegovina, Croatia, Macedonia, and Slovenia.

Sources: United Nations Statistical Office; The World Bank; *World Resources 1992–93.*

Part VII

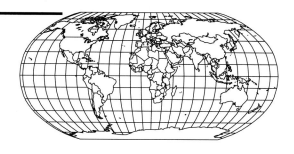

Military

Map 33 Nations With Nuclear Weapons

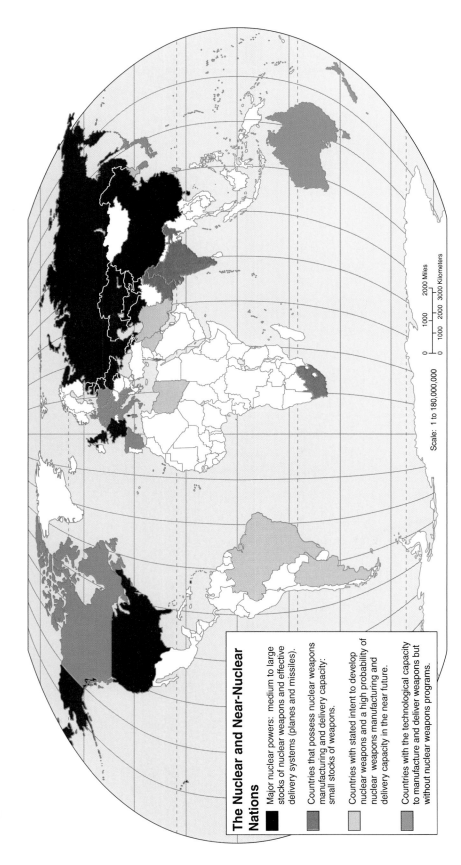

The Nuclear and Near-Nuclear Nations

■ Major nuclear powers: medium to large stocks of nuclear weapons and effective delivery systems (planes and missiles).

■ Countries that possess nuclear weapons manufacturing and delivery capacity: small stocks of weapons.

■ Countries with stated intent to develop nuclear weapons and a high probability of nuclear weapons manufacturing and delivery capacity in the near future.

■ Countries with the technological capacity to manufacture and deliver weapons but without nuclear weapons programs.

Scale: 1 to 180,000,000

```
0        1000        2000 Miles
0   1000   2000   3000 Kilometers
```

Since 1980 the number of countries possessing nuclear weapons manufacturing and delivery capacity has increased dramatically, increasing the chances of accidental nuclear exchanges. In addition to the traditional nuclear powers of France, the People's Republic of China, the former Soviet Union, the United Kingdom, and the United States, four other countries are now judged by many authorities to possess nuclear weapons capability. These four countries are: India, Israel, Pakistan, and South Africa. While the stockpile of weapons of these countries is small (ranging from a minimum of 5 to 10 weapons in Pakistan to a maximum of 50 to 200 weapons in Israel), the proliferation of countries capable of delivering nuclear warheads in time

of war is threatening to global security. In addition to the countries that already possess the capacity to make and deliver nuclear weapons, seven other countries have or recently have had active nuclear weapons programs and may possess nuclear weapons capacity by the year 2000. These countries include: Argentina, Brazil, Iran, Iraq, Libya, North Korea, and Taiwan. Finally, there are the countries—virtually all of them in the developed economies of the world—that possess the technological capacity to manufacture nuclear weapons and delivery systems but have chosen not to develop nuclear weapons programs. These countries include, among others, Australia, Canada, most western and eastern European countries, Japan, New Zealand, and South Korea.

Map 34 Military Expenditures as Percent of Total Central Government Expenditures

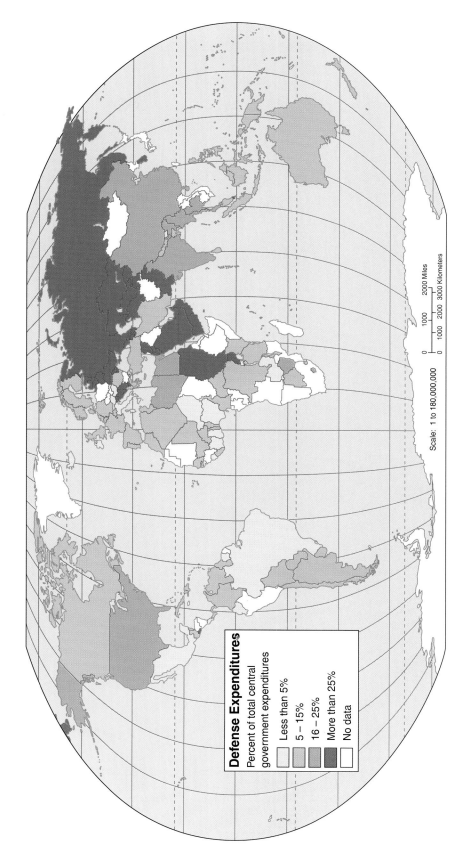

Defense Expenditures

Percent of total central government expenditures

- Less than 5%
- 5 – 15%
- 16 – 25%
- More than 25%
- No data

Scale: 1 to 180,000,000

0   1000   2000 Miles

0   1000   2000   3000 Kilometers

Many countries devote a significant amount of their total central governmental expenditures to defense: weapons, personnel, and research and development of military hardware. A glance at the map reveals those areas of the world where the expenditures for defense reflect the degree of past and present political tension between countries. The clearest example is the Middle East. One of the most alarming (and least well known) issues of military expenditure has to do with its consistent and steady increase in developing countries. In many of these countries, military expenditures have risen 7.5 percent per year for the past quarter-century. Even though many still spend less than 10 percent of their total central government expenditures on defense, it is money that could be put to different uses in such human development areas as housing, land reform, health care, and education.

Map 35 Size of Armed Forces

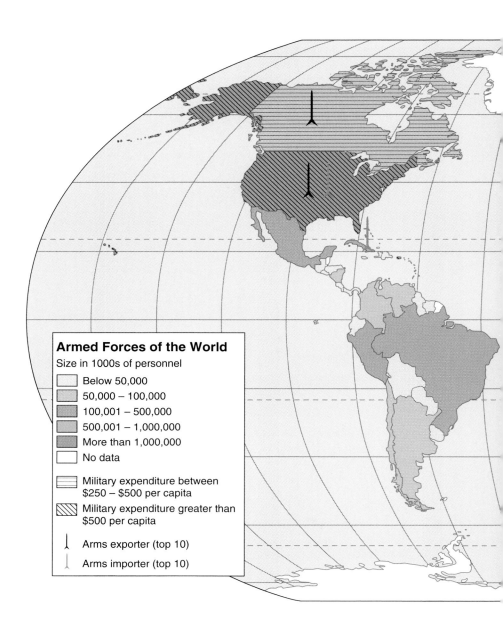

Armed Forces of the World

Size in 1000s of personnel

- Below 50,000
- 50,000 – 100,000
- 100,001 – 500,000
- 500,001 – 1,000,000
- More than 1,000,000
- No data

- Military expenditure between $250 – $500 per capita
- Military expenditure greater than $500 per capita

- Arms exporter (top 10)
- Arms importer (top 10)

While it is still an indicator of national power on the international scene, the size of a country's armed forces is no longer as important as it once was. The increasing high technology of military hardware allows smaller numbers of military personnel to be more effective. There are some countries, such as China, that have massive numbers of military personnel but relatively limited military power because of a lack of modern weaponry. Additionally, the use of rapid transportation allows personnel to be deployed about the globe or any region of it quickly; this also increases the effectiveness of highly trained and well-armed smaller military units. Nevertheless, the world is still a long way from the predicted "push-button warfare" that many experts have long antici-

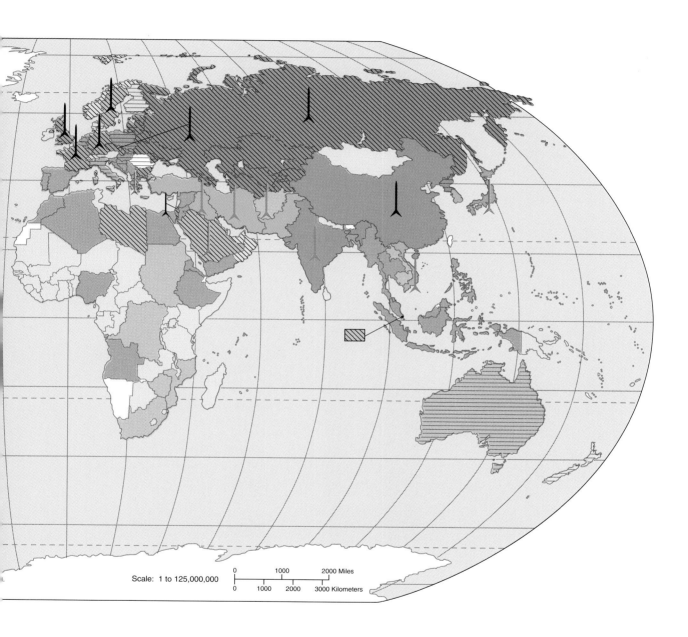

Scale: 1 to 125,000,000

| 0 | | 1000 | | 2000 Miles |
| 0 | 1000 | 2000 | 3000 Kilometers |

pated. Indeed, the pattern of the last few years has been for most military conflicts to involve ground troops engaged in fairly traditional patterns of operation. Even in the Persian Gulf conflict, with its highly publicized "smart bombs," the bulk of the military operation that ended the conflict was carried out by infantry and armor operating on the ground and supported by traditional air cover using conventional weaponry. Thus, while the size of a country's armed forces may not be as important as it once was, it is still a major factor in measuring the ability of nations to engage successfully in armed conflict.

Map 36 Alliance and Conflict in the Post-World War II World

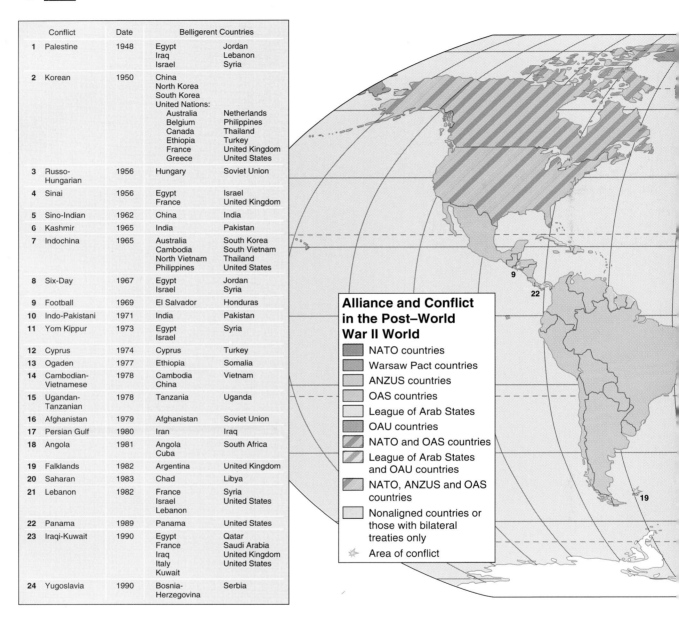

	Conflict	Date	Belligerent Countries	
1	Palestine	1948	Egypt Iraq Israel	Jordan Lebanon Syria

2	Korean	1950	China
			North Korea
			South Korea
			United Nations:
			  Australia
			  Belgium
			  Canada
			  Ethiopia
			  France
			  Greece
				
				Netherlands
				Philippines
				Thailand
				Turkey
				United Kingdom
				United States

3	Russo-Hungarian	1956	Hungary	Soviet Union
4	Sinai	1956	Egypt France	Israel United Kingdom
5	Sino-Indian	1962	China	India
6	Kashmir	1965	India	Pakistan
7	Indochina	1965	Australia Cambodia North Vietnam Philippines	South Korea South Vietnam Thailand United States
8	Six-Day	1967	Egypt Israel	Jordan Syria
9	Football	1969	El Salvador	Honduras
10	Indo-Pakistani	1971	India	Pakistan
11	Yom Kippur	1973	Egypt Israel	Syria
12	Cyprus	1974	Cyprus	Turkey
13	Ogaden	1977	Ethiopia	Somalia
14	Cambodian-Vietnamese	1978	Cambodia China	Vietnam
15	Ugandan-Tanzanian	1978	Tanzania	Uganda
16	Afghanistan	1979	Afghanistan	Soviet Union
17	Persian Gulf	1980	Iran	Iraq
18	Angola	1981	Angola Cuba	South Africa
19	Falklands	1982	Argentina	United Kingdom
20	Saharan	1983	Chad	Libya
21	Lebanon	1982	France Israel Lebanon	Syria United States
22	Panama	1989	Panama	United States
23	Iraqi-Kuwait	1990	Egypt France Iraq Italy Kuwait	Qatar Saudi Arabia United Kingdom United States
24	Yugoslavia	1990	Bosnia-Herzegovina	Serbia

Alliance and Conflict in the Post–World War II World

- NATO countries
- Warsaw Pact countries
- ANZUS countries
- OAS countries
- League of Arab States
- OAU countries
- NATO and OAS countries
- League of Arab States and OAU countries
- NATO, ANZUS and OAS countries
- Nonaligned countries or those with bilateral treaties only
- ✦ Area of conflict

Although the years since the end of World War II are often referred to as "the postwar era," in the years following 1945 there developed an elaborate international system of alliances based on potential or perceived military threats. The most important of these alliances were NATO (the North Atlantic Treaty Organization) and the Warsaw Pact (countries allied with the Soviet Union). Other alliances with at least some military implications include: ANZUS (Australia, New Zealand, the United States), OAS (the Organization of American States), the League of Arab States, and OAU (the Organization of African Unity). Since 1992, the Warsaw Pact has ceased to exist, leaving NATO as the only major military alliance in the world. During the same time frame (1945–1992) that NATO and the Warsaw Pact dominated global military policy-making, there have also been numerous conflicts involving military forces of belligerent countries that were neither NATO nor Warsaw Pact members. Most of these conflicts have inflicted heavy damage to the environment and to civilian populations, as well as

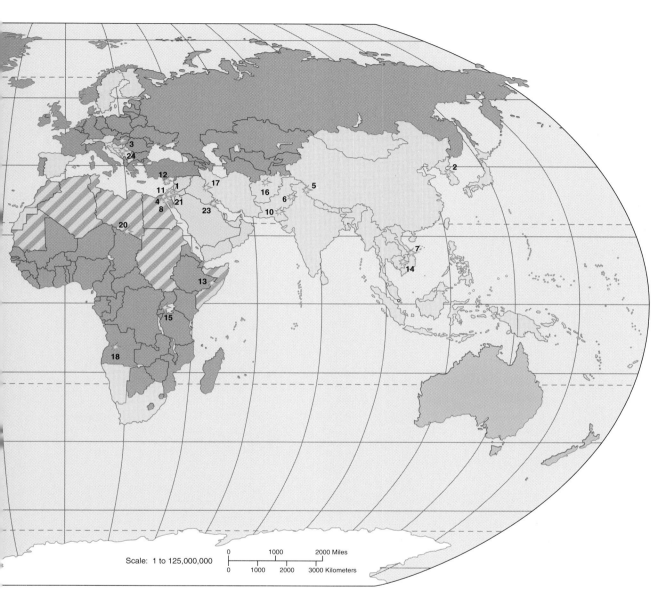

Scale: 1 to 125,000,000

0   1000   2000 Miles

0   1000   2000   3000 Kilometers

casualties among the participating military forces. Many of the conflicts shown on the map were not wars in the traditional sense of two or more countries formally declaring war, severing diplomatic ties, and devoting their entire national energies to the war effort (as was the case with most belligerent nations in World War II). Rather, many of these conflicts were undeclared wars, often fought between rival groups within the same country with outside support from other countries. Thus, many of the conflicts can be characterized as civil wars, insurgencies, or wars produced by irredentism or separatist groups within a country. The Afghan war, for example, was fought between the formal government of Afghanistan and rebellious or insurgency forces, with the Soviet Union coming to the aid of the formal government. Similarly, the Vietnam war was really a civil war between rival factions for control of Vietnam, with the United States entering the conflict in support of the southern Vietnamese.

Table I

Military Arms Transfers, 1985–1989: Major Recipients and Suppliers

RECIPIENT COUNTRIES	VALUE OF ARMS TRANSFERS (cumulative: millions of $)	MAJOR SUPPLIERS[1] (in order of importance)
Saudi Arabia	23,040	United Kingdom, France, United States, China, Latin America
Iraq	22,750	Soviet Union, other Warsaw Pact, China, France, Latin America
India	16,080	Soviet Union, France, United Kingdom, other Europe,[2] other Warsaw Pact
Iran	10,250	Other Europe, China, other East Asia, other Warsaw Pact
United States	9,930	United Kingdom, others, France, other Europe, West Germany
Afghanistan	9,730	Soviet Union
Cuba	8,690	Soviet Union, other Warsaw Pact
Vietnam	8,250	Soviet Union
Syria	7,160	Soviet Union, other Warsaw Pact
Israel	6,100	United States
Angola	6,000	Soviet Union, other Warsaw Pact, France
Soviet Union	5,910	Other Warsaw Pact
Egypt	5,800	United States, France, other Europe, Soviet Union, other Warsaw Pact
Japan	5,490	United States, United Kingdom
Libya	5,080	Soviet Union, other Warsaw Pact, other Europe
Poland	4,780	Soviet Union, other Warsaw Pact
Australia	4,550	United States, other Europe, United Kingdom
East Germany	4,425	Soviet Union, other Warsaw Pact
Turkey	3,970	United States, West Germany, United Kingdom, other Europe
Taiwan	3,885	United States, other Europe
Ethiopia	3,805	Soviet Union, other East Asia[3]
Bulgaria	3,600	Soviet Union, other Warsaw Pact
West Germany	3,530	United States, Middle East, France
Czechoslovakia	3,440	Soviet Union, other Warsaw Pact
Spain	3,335	United States, other Europe, United Kingdom
Algeria	3,260	Soviet Union, other Warsaw Pact
Greece	3,210	United States, France, West Germany
United Kingdom	3,200	United States
Korea, North	2,770	Soviet Union
Korea, South	2,645	United States
Netherlands	2,560	United States, West Germany
Nicaragua	2,390	Soviet Union, other Warsaw Pact
Switzerland	2,210	West Germany, United States, United Kingdom
China	2,205	Soviet Union, Middle East, United Kingdom, United States
Jordan	2,070	Soviet Union, United States, France, other Europe
Pakistan	2,000	United States, China, other Europe, France
North Yemen	1,765	Soviet Union, Middle East, other Warsaw Pact
Cambodia	1,580	Soviet Union, other East Asia
United Arab Emirates	1,495	France, United States, other Europe
Belgium	1,460	United States, France
Thailand	1,430	United States, China, West Germany
South Yemen	1,400	Soviet Union
Norway	1,275	United States, other Europe, West Germany
Kuwait	1,345	France, Middle East, Soviet Union, United States
Italy	1,220	United States
Singapore	1,105	United States, France
France	980	United States, other Europe
Venezuela	920	United States, other Europe, France, United Kingdom
Brazil	845	United States, France, West Germany
Yugoslavia	855	Soviet Union, United States

[1]Supplied minimum of 5% of total value of arms transfer during five-year period.

[2]Does not include France, United Kingdom, West Germany.

[3]Does not include China.

Source: World Military Expenditures and Arms (U.S. Government Printing Office, 1992).

Part VIII

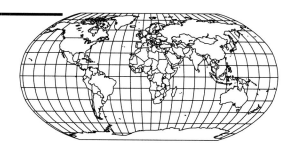

Environmental Conditions

Map 37 Deforestation and Desertification

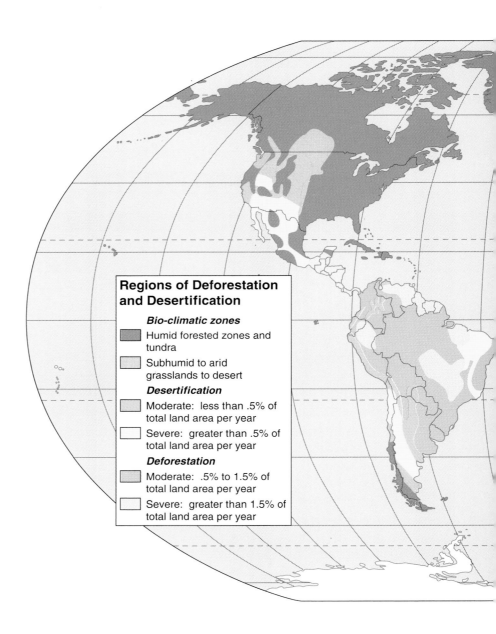

Regions of Deforestation and Desertification

Bio-climatic zones

- Humid forested zones and tundra
- Subhumid to arid grasslands to desert

Desertification

- Moderate: less than .5% of total land area per year
- Severe: greater than .5% of total land area per year

Deforestation

- Moderate: .5% to 1.5% of total land area per year
- Severe: greater than 1.5% of total land area per year

While those of us in the developed countries of the world tend to think of environmental deterioration as the consequence of our heavily industrialized economies, in fact the worst examples of current environmental degradation are to be found within the world's less developed regions. There, high population growth rates and economies limited primarily to farming have forced the increasing use of more marginal (less suited to cultivation) land. In the world's grassland and arid environments, which occupy approximately 40 percent of the world's total land area, increasing pressures of cultivation are turning vulnerable areas into deserts incapable of sustaining agricul-

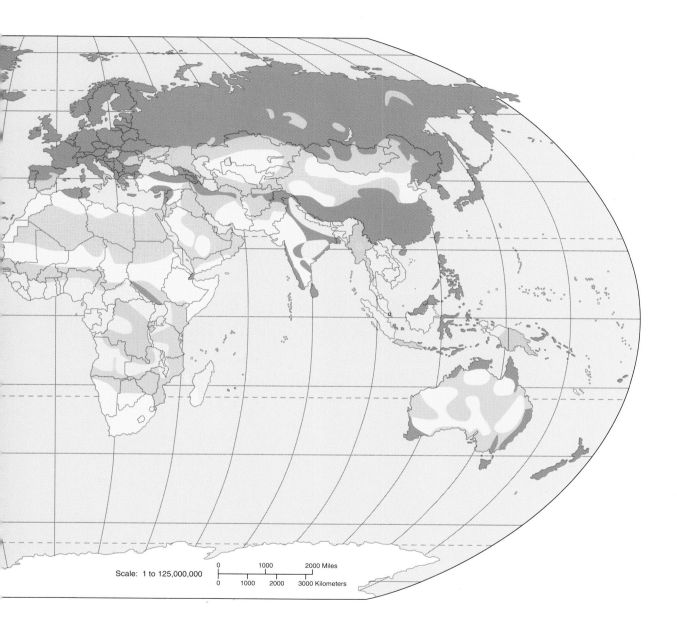

Scale: 1 to 125,000,000

0   1000   2000 Miles

0   1000   2000   3000 Kilometers

tural productivity. In the world's forested regions, particularly in the tropical forests of Latin America, Africa, and Asia, a similar process is occurring: increasing pressure for more farmland is creating a process of deforestation that destroys the soil, reduces the biological diversity of the forest regions, and—ultimately—may have the capacity to alter the global climate by contributing to an increase in carbon dioxide in the atmosphere. This increases the heat trapped in the atmosphere and enhances the greenhouse effect.

Map **38** Soil Erosion

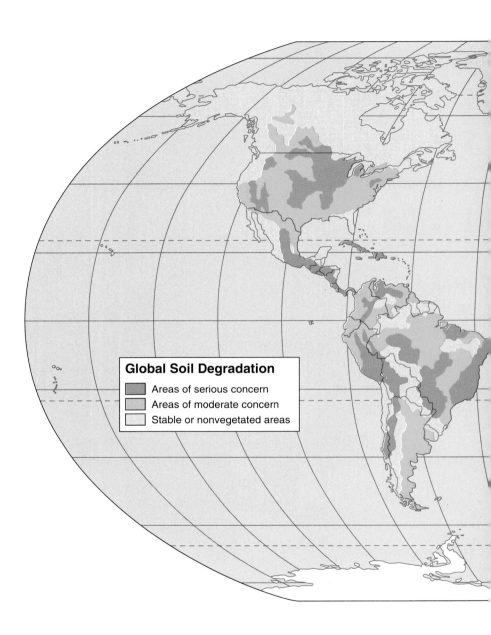

Global Soil Degradation

- Areas of serious concern
- Areas of moderate concern
- Stable or nonvegetated areas

Recent research has shown that more than 3 billion acres of the world's surface suffer from serious soil degradation, with more than 22 million acres so severely eroded or poisoned with chemicals that they can no longer support productive crop agriculture. Most of this soil damage has been caused by poor farming practices, overgrazing of domestic livestock, and deforestation. These activities strip away the protective cover of natural vegetation—forests and grasslands—allowing wind and water erosion to remove the topsoil that contains the necessary nutrients and soil microbes for plant growth. But millions of acres of topsoil have been degraded by chemicals as well. In some instances these chemicals are the result of overapplication of fertilizers, herbi-

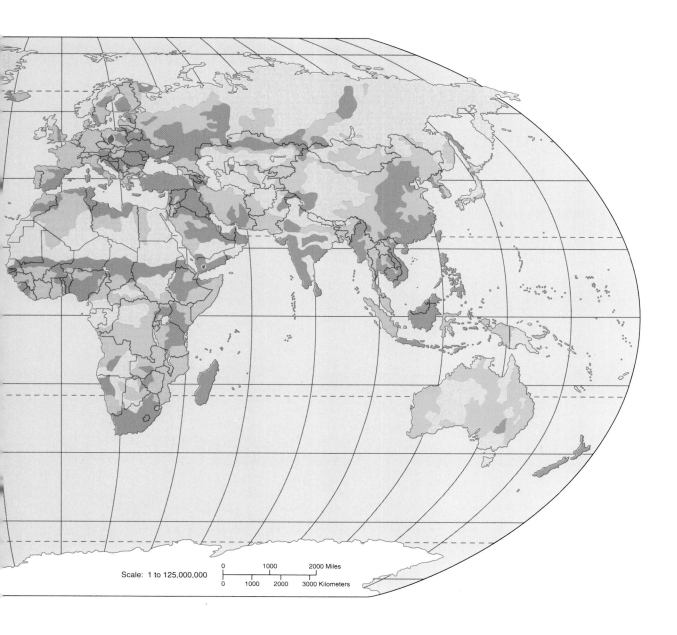

Scale: 1 to 125,000,000

cides, pesticides, and other agricultural chemicals. In other instances, chemical deposition from industrial and urban wastes and from acid precipitation have poisoned millions of acres of soil. As the map shows, soil erosion and pollution are not just a problem in developing countries with high population densities and increasing use of marginal lands. They are equally a problem in the more highly developed regions of mechanized, industrial agriculture. While many methods for preventing or reducing soil degradation exist, they are seldom used because of ignorance, cost, or perceived economic inefficiency.

Map 39 Air and Water Quality

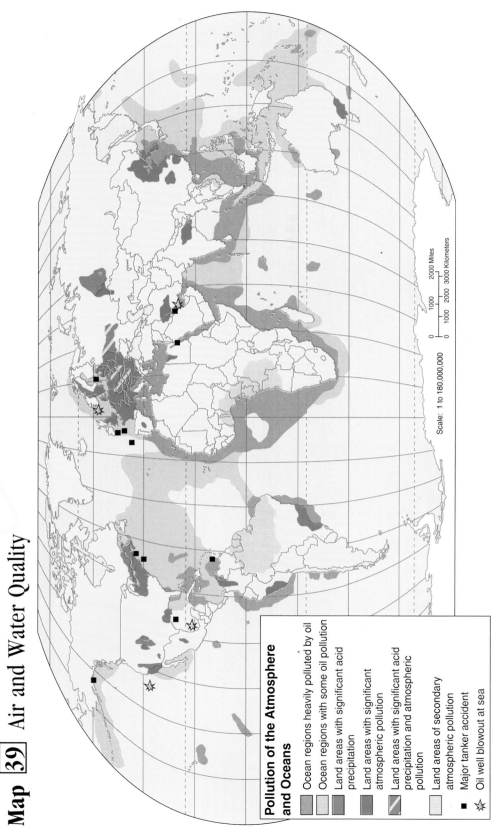

Pollution of the Atmosphere and Oceans

- Ocean regions heavily polluted by oil
- Ocean regions with some oil pollution
- Land areas with significant acid precipitation
- Land areas with significant atmospheric pollution
- Land areas with significant acid precipitation and atmospheric pollution
- Land areas of secondary atmospheric pollution
- ■ Major tanker accident
- ☆ Oil well blowout at sea

Scale: 1 to 180,000,000

0   1000   2000 Miles
0 1000 2000 3000 Kilometers

The pollution of the world's oceans and atmosphere has long been a matter of concern to environmental scientists. The great circulation systems of ocean and air are the controlling factors of the Earth's natural environment, and modifications to those systems have unknown consequences. This map is based on what we can measure: (1) areas of oceans where oil pollution has been proven to have inflicted significant damage to ocean ecosystems and life-forms (including phytoplankton—the oceans' primary food producers, the marine equivalent of land vegetation); (2) areas of oceans where unusually high concentrations of hydrocarbons from oil spills may have inflicted some damage to the oceans' biota; (3) land areas where the combination of sulphur and nitrogen oxides with atmospheric water vapor has produced acid precipi-

tation at high enough levels to have produced significant damage to terrestrial vegetation systems; (4) land areas where the emissions from industrial, transportation, commercial, residential, and other uses of fossil fuels have produced concentrations of atmospheric pollutants high enough to be damaging to human health; and (5) land areas of "secondary" air pollution where the primary pollutant is smoke from forest clearance. A glance at the map shows that there are few areas of the world where some form of oceanic or atmospheric pollution is not a part of our environmental system. The long-range implications of this pollution are still being debated by scientists—but nearly all agree that the consequences, whatever they may be, will not be good.

Map ④⓪ Per Capita CO₂ Emissions

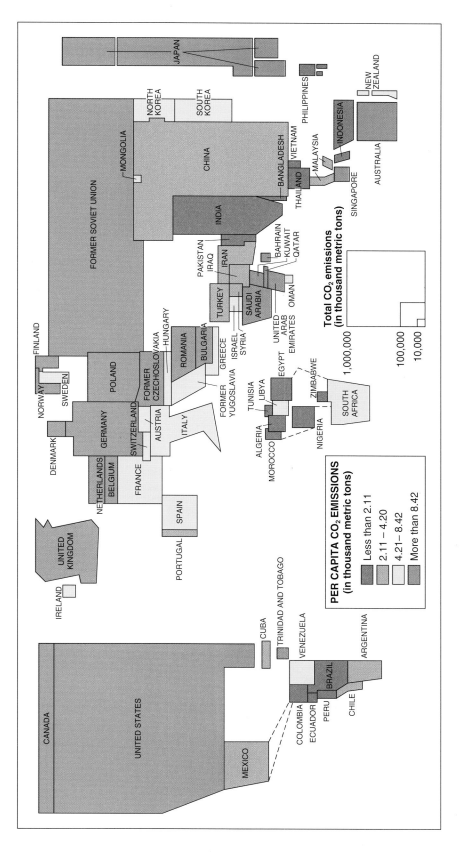

PER CAPITA CO₂ EMISSIONS
(in thousand metric tons)

- Less than 2.11
- 2.11 – 4.20
- 4.21 – 8.42
- More than 8.42

Total CO₂ emissions
(in thousand metric tons)

1,000,000

100,000

10,000

Carbon dioxide emissions are a major indicator of economic development, since they are generated largely by burning of fossil fuels for electrical power generation, for industrial processes, for domestic and commercial heating, and for the internal combustion engines of automobiles, trucks, buses, planes, and trains. Most scientists are now in agreement that carbon dioxide in the atmosphere increases the ability of the atmosphere to retain heat and is thus respon-

sible for global warming and a potential worldwide change of climate patterns. These climatological changes threaten disaster for many regions and their peoples in both the developed and lesser-developed areas of the world. You will note from the cartogram that the countries of the Northern Hemisphere generate extremely high levels of carbon dioxide per capita.

Table J
Forest Resources by Region

	EXTENT OF FOREST, 1980 (in thousands of hectares)				ANNUAL DEFORESTATION, 1980–1985	
	CLOSED FOREST[1]	OPEN FOREST[2]	PLANTATION[3]	OTHER[4]	THOUSANDS OF HECTARES	% OF TOTAL
WORLD	2,822,560	742,148	28,830	1,695,017	11,502	0.3
AFRICA	222,278	483,911	2,971	629,900	3,772	0.5
North Africa	3,371	2,119	1,062	3,775	58	1.1
West Sahelian Africa	2,345	39,609	47	51,123	388	0.9
East Sahelian Africa	8,412	83,863	524	226,799	695	0.8
West Africa	17,267	36,306	327	104,960	1,199	2.2
Central Africa	170,395	111,915	76	71,575	575	0.2
Tropical Southern Africa	8,818	207,109	556	161,574	700	0.3
Temperate Southern Africa	1,351	70	102	2,803	X	X
Insular Africa	10,319	2,900	277	7,561	157	1.2
THE AMERICAS	1,212,849	207,172	6,175	590,871	5,702	0.4
Temperate North America	490,554	X	X	243,922	X	X
Central America and Mexico	64,929	2,560	183	91,524	1,022	1.5
Caribbean Subregion	37,066	482	205	3,055	26	0.1
Nontropical South America	52,540	X	1,557	25,170	50	0.1
Tropical South America	567,760	204,130	4,320	227,200	4,604	0.6
ASIA	424,713	47,103	19,605	176,994	2,003	0.4
Temperate and Middle East Asia	153,755	20,100	14,515	70,040	20	0.0
South Asia	60,653	5,908	2,494	17,906	307	0.5
Continental South East Asia	65,904	18,905	352	39,440	709	0.8
Insular South East Asia	144,401	3,000	2,244	49,608	967	0.7
EUROPE	136,652	X	X	41,688	X	X
COMMONWEALTH OF INDEPENDENT STATES	739,900	X	X	189,700	X	X
OCEANIA	86,168	3,962	79	65,864	26	0.0

[1]Closed forest is land where trees cover a high proportion of the ground surface and where grass does not form a continuous cover on the forest floor.

[2]Open forest consists of mixed forest and grasslands with at least 10% forest cover.

[3]Plantations are forest stands maintained artificially by afforestation and reforestation for industrial and nonindustrial use.

[4]Other wooded area encompasses forest fallows and shrubs in tropical countries and, in the temperate zones, forests with 5%–20% of their area covered by tree crowns or areas where shrubs or stunted trees cover more than 20% of their area.

Sources: Food and Agriculture Organization of the United Nations; United Nations Economic Commission for Europe; *World Resources 1992–93.*

Table K

Human-Induced Soil Destruction 1945–1990

	TOTAL DEGRADED AREA[1] (millions of hectares)	DEGRADED AREA AS % OF VEGETATED LAND[2]	EROSION[3] (millions of hectares)		DEGRADATION[4] (millions of hectares)	
			WATER	WIND	CHEMICAL	PHYSICAL
WORLD	**1,964.4**	**17**	**1,093.7**	**548.3**	**239.1**	**83.3**
Light Degradation	749.0	6	343.2	268.6	93.0	44.2
Moderate Degradation	910.5	8	526.7	253.6	103.3	26.8
Strong Degradation	295.7	3	217.2	24.3	41.9	12.3
Extreme Degradation	9.3	0	6.6	1.9	0.8	0.0
AFRICA	**494.2**	**22**	**227.4**	**186.5**	**61.5**	**18.7**
Light Degradation	173.6	8	57.5	88.3	26.0	1.8
Moderate Degradation	191.8	9	67.4	89.3	27.0	8.1
Strong Degradation	123.6	6	98.3	7.9	8.6	8.8
Extreme Degradation	5.2	0	4.2	1.0	0.0	0.0
NORTH AND CENTRAL AMERICA	**158.1**	**8**	**106.1**	**39.2**	**7.0**	**5.9**
Light Degradation	18.9	1	14.5	2.6	0.5	1.3
Moderate Degradation	112.5	5	68.2	34.9	5.7	3.8
Strong Degradation	26.7	1	23.4	1.7	0.8	0.8
Extreme Degradation	0.0	0	0.0	0.0	0.0	0.0
SOUTH AMERICA	**243.4**	**14**	**123.2**	**41.9**	**70.3**	**7.9**
Light Degradation	104.8	6	45.9	25.8	26.3	6.8
Moderate Degradation	113.5	7	65.1	16.1	31.4	0.8
Strong Degradation	25.0	1	12.1	0.0	12.6	0.3
Extreme Degradation	0.0	0	0.0	0.0	0.0	
ASIA[5]	**748.0**	**20**	**440.6**	**222.2**	**73.2**	**12.1**
Light Degradation	294.5	8	124.5	132.4	31.8	5.7
Moderate Degradation	344.3	9	241.7	75.1	21.5	6.0
Strong Degradation	107.7	3	73.4	14.5	19.5	0.4
Extreme Degradation	0.5	0	0.0	0.2	0.4	0.0
EUROPE	**218.9**	**23**	**114.5**	**42.2**	**25.8**	**36.4**
Light Degradation	60.6	6	21.4	3.2	8.1	27.9
Moderate Degradation	144.4	15	81.0	38.2	17.1	8.1
Strong Degradation	10.7	1	9.8	0.0	0.6	0.4
Extreme Degradation	3.1	0	2.4	0.7	0.0	0.0
OCEANIA	**102.9**	**13**	**82.8**	**16.4**	**1.3**	**2.3**
Light Degradation	96.6	12	79.4	16.3	0.2	0.7
Moderate Degradation	3.9	0	3.2	0.0	0.7	0.0
Strong Degradation	1.9	0	0.2	0.1	0.0	1.6
Extreme Degradation	0.4	0	0.0	0.0	0.4	0.0

[1]Degraded soils are those in which the current and/or future capacity to produce goods and services has been lowered.

[2]Vegetated land includes all natural vegetated areas and all agricultural land.

[3]Erosion is topsoil loss, the removal of soil by wind action, surface wash, or sheet erosion.

[4]Degradation includes both chemical and physical soil deterioration. Chemical degradation includes nutrient loss from overcultivation, salinization from irrigation, pollution from agricultural chemicals and other sources, and acidification from overfertilization or acid precipitation. Physical degradation includes compaction from livestock or heavy machinery, waterlogging through overirrigation or drainage disturbances, and subsidence by drainage disturbance or oxidation.

[5]European Russia and the Commonwealth states east of the Ural Mountains (Belarus, Moldova, Ukraine, Armenia, and Azerbaijan) are included in values for Europe; Siberia and Asian Russia and the Commonwealth states west of the Urals (Kazakhstan, Uzbekistan, Tajikistan, Turkmenistan, and Kyrgyzstan) are included in the values for Asia.

Sources: United Nations Environmental Programme; International Soil Reference and Information Centre; *World Resources 1992–93.*

Table L

Water Resources, 1990

	ANNUAL RENEWABLE WATER RESOURCES[1]		ANNUAL WITHDRAWALS[2]		
	TOTAL (km^3)	PER CAPITA (thousands of m^3)	TOTAL (km^3)	% OF RESOURCES	PER CAPITA (m^3)
WORLD	**40,673**	**7.69**	**3,240**	**8**	**660**
AFRICA	**4,184**	**6.46**	**144**	**3**	**244**
Algeria	18.9	0.75	3.00	16	161
Angola	158	15.77	0.48	0	43
Benin	26	5.48	0.11	0	26
Botswana	1	0.78	0.09	1	98
Burkina Faso	28	3.11	0.15	1	20
Burundi	3.6	0.66	0.10	3	20
Cameroon	208	18.50	0.40	0	30
Cape Verde	0.20	0.53	0.04	20	148
Central African Republic	141	48.40	0.07	0	27
Chad	38.4	6.76	0.18	0	35
Comoros	1.02	1.97	0.01	1	15
Congo	181	90.77	0.04	0	20
Djibouti	0.30	0.74	0.01	2	28
Egypt	1.80	0.03	56.40	97	1,202
Equatorial Guinea	30	68.18	0.01	0	11
Ethiopia	110	2.35	2.21	2	48
Gabon	164	140.05	0.06	0	51
Gambia	3	3.50	0.02	0	33
Ghana	53	3.53	0.30	1	35
Guinea	226	32.87	0.74	0	115
Guinea-Bissau	31	31.41	0.01	0	18
Ivory Coast	74	5.87	0.71	1	68
Kenya	14.8	0.59	1.09	7	48
Lesotho	4	2.25	0.05	1	34
Liberia	232	90.84	0.13	0	54
Libya	0.70	0.15	2.83	404	623
Madagascar	40	3.34	16.30	41	1,675
Malawi	9	1.07	0.16	2	22
Mali	62	6.62	1.36	2	159
Mauritania	0.40	0.20	0.73	10	473
Mauritius	2.2	1.99	0.36	16	415
Morocco	30	1.19	11.00	37	501
Mozambique	58	3.70	0.76	1	53
Namibia	9	X	0.14	2	77
Niger	14	1.97	0.29	1	44
Nigeria	261	2.31	3.63	1	44
Rwanda	6.3	0.87	0.15	2	23
Senegal	23.2	3.15	1.36	4	201
Sierra Leone	160	38.54	0.37	0	99
Somalia	11.5	1.52	0.81	7	167
South Africa	50	1.42	9.20	18	404
Sudan	30	1.19	18.60	14	1,089
Swaziland	6.96	8.82	0.29	4	414
Tanzania	76	2.78	0.48	1	36
Togo	11.5	3.33	0.09	1	40
Tunisia	3.75	0.46	2.30	53	325
Uganda	66	3.58	0.20	0	20
Zaire	1,019	28.31	0.70	0	22
Zambia	96	11.35	0.36	0	86
Zimbabwe	23	2.37	1.22	5	129
NORTH AND CENTRAL AMERICA	**6,945**	**16.26**	**697**	**10**	**1,692**
Barbados	0.05	0.20	0.03	51	117

	ANNUAL RENEWABLE WATER RESOURCES[1]		ANNUAL WITHDRAWALS[2]		
	TOTAL (km³)	PER CAPITA (thousands of m³)	TOTAL (km³)	% OF RESOURCES	PER CAPITA (m³)
Belize	16	X	0.02	0	X
Canada	2,901	109.37	42.20	1	1,752
Costa Rica	95	31.51	1.35	1	779
Cuba	34.5	3.34	8.10	23	868
Dominican Republic	20	2.79	2.97	15	453
El Salvador	18.95	3.61	1	5	241
Guatemala	116	12.61	0.73	1	139
Haiti	11	1.69	0.04	0	46
Honduras	102	19.85	1.34	1	508
Jamaica	8.3	3.29	0.32	4	157
Mexico	357.4	4.03	54.20	15	901
Nicaragua	175	45.21	0.89	1	370
Panama	144	59.55	1.30	1	744
Trinidad and Tobago	5.1	3.98	0.15	3	149
United States	2,478	9.94	467	19	2,162
SOUTH AMERICA	**10,377**	**34.96**	**133**	**1**	**476**
Argentina	694	21.47	27.60	3	1,059
Bolivia	300	41.02	1.24	0	184
Brazil	5,190	34.52	35.04	1	212
Chile	468	35.53	16.80	4	1,625
Colombia	1,070	33.63	5.34	0	179
Ecuador	314	29.12	5.56	2	561
Guyana	241	231.73	5.40	2	7,616
Paraguay	94	21.98	0.43	0	111
Peru	40	1.79	6.10	15	294
Suriname	200	496.28	0.46	0	1,181
Uruguay	59	18.86	0.65	1	241
Venezuela	856	43.37	4.10	0	387
ASIA	**10,485**	**3.37**	**1,531**	**15**	**526**
Afghanistan	50	3.02	26.11	52	1,436
Bahrain	0	0	.31	X	609
Bangladesh	1,357	11.74	22.50	1	211
Bhutan	95	62.66	0.02	0	15
Cambodia	88.1	10.68	0.52	0	69
China	2,800	2.47	460	16	462
Cyprus	0.90	1.28	0.54	60	807
India	1,850	2.17	380	18	612
Indonesia	2,530	14.02	16.59	1	96
Iran	117.5	2.08	45.40	39	1,362
Iraq	34	1.80	42.80	43	4,575
Israel	1.7	0.37	1.90	88	447
Japan	547	4.43	107.8	20	923
Jordan	0.70	0.16	0.45	41	173
Korea, North	67	2.92	14.16	21	1,649
Korea, South	63	1.45	10.70	17	298
Kuwait	0	0	.5	X	238
Laos	270	66.32	0.99	0	228
Lebanon	4.8	1.62	0.75	16	271
Malaysia	456	26.30	9.42	2	765
Mongolia	24.6	11.05	0.55	2	272
Myanmar	1,082	25.96	3.96	0	103
Nepal	170	8.88	2.68	2	155
Oman	2	1.36	0.48	24	325
Pakistan	298	2.43	153.40	33	2,053
Philippines	323	5.18	29.50	9	693
Qatar	0.02	0.06	0.15	663	415
Saudi Arabia	2.2	0.16	3.60	164	255
Singapore	0.6	0.22	0.19	32	84
Sri Lanka	43.2	2.51	6.30	15	503
Syria	7.6	0.61	3.34	9	449

(continued on next page)

	ANNUAL RENEWABLE WATER RESOURCES[1]		ANNUAL WITHDRAWALS[2]		
	TOTAL (km^3)	PER CAPITA (thousands of m^3)	TOTAL (km^3)	% OF RESOURCES	PER CAPITA (m^3)
Thailand	110	1.97	31.9	18	599
Turkey	196	3.52	15.60	8	317
United Arab Emirates	0.3	0.19	0.9	299	565
Vietnam	376	5.6	5.07	1	81
Yemen	2.5	0.23	3.4	141	X
EUROPE	**2,321**	**4.66**	**359**	**15**	**726**
Albania	10	3.08	0.20	1	94
Austria	56.3	7.51	3.13	3	417
Belgium	8.4	0.85	9.03	72	917
Bulgaria	18	2	14.18	7	1,600
Czechoslovakia[3]	28	1.79	5.80	6	379
Denmark	11	2.15	1.46	11	289
Finland	110	22.11	3.70	3	774
France	170	3.03	40	22	728
Germany	96	1.23	50.35	26	643
Greece	45.15	4.49	6.95	12	721
Hungary	6	0.57	5.38	5	502
Iceland	170	671.94	0.09	0	349
Ireland	50	13.44	0.79	2	267
Italy	179.4	3.13	56.2	30	983
Luxembourg	1	2.72	0.04	1	119
Malta	0.03	0.07	0.02	92	68
Netherlands	10	0.68	14.47	16	1,023
Norway	405	96.15	2	0	489
Poland	49.4	1.29	16.80	30	472
Portugal	34	3.31	10.50	16	1,062
Romania	37	1.59	25.40	12	1,144
Spain	110.3	2.80	45.25	41	1,174
Sweden	176	21.11	3.98	2	479
Switzerland	42.5	6.52	3.2	6	502
United Kingdom	120	2.11	28.35	24	507
U.S.S.R.[4]	4,384	15.22	353	8	1,330
Yugoslavia[5]	150	6.29	8.77	3	393
OCEANIA	**2,011**	**75.96**	**23**	**1**	**907**
Australia	343	20.48	17.8	5	1,306
Fiji	28.55	38.12	0.03	0	37
New Zealand	397	117.49	1.20	0	379
Papua New Guinea	801	199.70	0.10	0	25
Solomon Islands	44.7	149	0	0	18

[1]Annual internal renewable water resources refer to the average annual flow of rivers plus annual groundwater recharge from precipitation.

[2]Annual withdrawals refer to the total use of water, not including evaporation losses from storage reservoirs and soil and transpiration loss from vegetation. Water withdrawals also include water from desalinization plants in countries where that use is a significant part of all water withdrawals.

[3]On January 1, 1993, Czechoslovakia was separated by peaceful agreement into two independent countries, the Czech Republic and the Slovak Republic. At the time of this printing, information was not yet available for these two separate countries.

[4]At the time of this printing, separate statistical data on the countries of the Commonwealth of Independent States were not yet available, nor were there available data on the former Soviet republics that are not members of the C.I.S. The data for the former U.S.S.R. thus include information for Russia and the other Commonwealth countries of Armenia, Azerbaijan, Belarus, Kazakhstan, Kyrgyzstan, Moldova, Tajikistan, Turkmenistan, Ukraine, and Uzbekistan, along with the non-Commonwealth countries of Estonia, Georgia, Latvia, and Lithuania.

[5]At the time of this printing, separate statistical data on the countries that made up the former state of Yugoslavia were not yet available. The data for Yugoslavia thus include information for the Federal Republic of Yugoslavia (Serbia and Montenegro) and the independent countries of Bosnia-Herzegovina, Croatia, Macedonia, and Slovenia.

Sources: Bureau of Geological Research and Mining; National Geological Survey, France; Institute of Geography; National Academy of Sciences, Russia; Eurostat; International Desalinization Association; *World Resources 1992–93.*

Table M

Greenhouse Gas Emissions, 1990[1] (in metric tons)

	INDUSTRIAL CO$_2$[2]	LAND USE CO$_2$[3]	METHANE[4]	CFCs[5]
WORLD	21,863,088	6,400,00	270,000	580
AFRICA	647,362	1,500,000	19,000	16
Algeria	46,492	X	970	1
Angola	4,965	33,000	340	X
Benin	667	9,500	54	X
Botswana	1,700	2,600	97	X
Burkina Faso	520	17,000	170	X
Burundi	176	530	34	X
Cameroon	5,774	60,000	230	X
Cape Verde	77	X	2	X
Central African Republic	264	13,000	100	X
Chad	202	15,000	220	X
Comoros	51	X	11	X
Congo	1,773	12,000	21	X
Djibouti	326	X	11	X
Egypt	79,483	X	670	3
Equatorial Guinea	106	1,800	1	X
Ethiopia	2,565	30,000	1,400	X
Gabon	7,826	9,300	170	0
Gambia	183	1,900	18	X
Ghana	3,521	31,000	120	1
Guinea	1,000	37,000	300	X
Guinea-Bissau	147	18,000	72	X
Ivory Coast	7,995	350,000	200	1
Kenya	5,192	13,000	640	0
Lesotho	0	X	X	X
Liberia	773	39,000	63	0
Libya	37,842	X	290	X
Madagascar	901	120,000	860	0
Malawi	634	58,000	73	X
Mali	425	7,700	310	X
Mauritania	3,023	X	140	X
Mauritius	1,000	X	4	X
Morocco	22,120	X	310	1
Mozambique	1,205	30,000	130	X
Namibia	0	X	X	X
Niger	1,008	7,400	230	X
Nigeria	79,263	270,000	3,700	0
Rwanda	381	2,100	46	0
Senegal	3,151	11,000	160	0
Sierra Leone	671	4,600	97	X
Somalia	960	5,200	760	X
South Africa	278,468	X	3,400	7
Sudan	3,338	98,000	1,200	X
Swaziland	443	X	27	X
Tanzania	2,009	21,000	740	X
Togo	627	2,900	34	0
Tunisia	13,923	X	90	0
Uganda	879	10,000	210	X
Zaire	3,822	130,000	290	X
Zambia	2,612	27,000	120	X
Zimbabwe	16,059	16,000	310	1
NORTH AND CENTRAL AMERICA	5,760,830	420,000	45,000	150
Barbados	971	X	2	0
Belize	180	X	2	X
Canada	455,530	X	4,100	11
Costa Rica	2,557	26,000	78	0

(continued on next page)

	INDUSTRIAL CO$_2$[2]	LAND USE CO$_2$[3]	METHANE[4]	CFCs[5]
Cuba	36,292	890	310	0
Dominican Republic	6,745	1,300	160	0
El Salvador	2,352	1,600	59	0
Guatemala	4,071	41,000	110	1
Haiti	725	860	90	X
Honduras	1,979	42,000	110	0
Jamaica	4,899	810	18	1
Mexico	319,702	200,000	2,300	5
Nicaragua	2,180	59,000	87	0
Panama	2,730	19,000	75	0
Trinidad and Tobago	18,580	330	470	0
United States	4,869,005	22,000	37,000	130
SOUTH AMERICA	557,296	1,800,000	18,000	15
Argentina	118,157	X	3,800	3
Bolivia	5,064	37,000	360	0
Brazil	206,957	950,000	8,800	6
Chile	31,833	X	270	0
Colombia	53,831	420,000	1,500	2
Ecuador	15,316	160,000	330	0
Guyana	660	1,100	27	X
Paraguay	1,722	67,000	310	0
Peru	21,174	140,000	330	0
Suriname	1,440	1,100	43	0
Uruguay	4,749	X	530	0
Venezuela	95,887	59,000	1,400	2
ASIA	5,812,064	2,600,000	130,000	140
Afghanistan	6,273	X	480	X
Bahrain	12,161	X	79	0
Bangladesh	14,114	8,700	6,900	X
Bhutan	33	860	40	X
Cambodia	451	11,000	1,100	X
China	2,388,613	X	40,000	12
Cyprus	4,192	X	6	0
India	651,936	120,000	36,000	4
Indonesia	137,726	870,000	6,500	1
Iran	166,074	X	1,500	3
Iraq	68,898	X	950	1
Israel	32,903	X	140	3
Japan	1,040,554	X	4,100	95
Jordan	9,416	X	17	1
Korea, North	151,488	X	1,200	X
Korea, South	221,104	X	1,200	5
Kuwait	31,181	X	250	1
Laos	227	240,000	370	X
Lebanon	8,720	X	10	X
Malaysia	49,061	280,000	890	2
Mongolia	10,303	X	260	X
Myanmar	5,009	380,000	3,200	X
Nepal	934	32,000	1,000	X
Oman	10,259	X	150	X
Pakistan	60,973	4,000	3,400	6
Philippines	40,960	190,000	2,400	1
Qatar	13,308	X	88	X
Saudi Arabia	173,776	X	1,100	3
Singapore	35,880	X	7	1
Sri Lanka	4,034	22,000	540	0
Syria	28,154	X	190	1
Thailand	77,680	290,000	6,300	3
Turkey	126,078	X	880	1
United Arab Emirates	50,944	X	480	1
Vietnam	18,170	150,000	3,600	X
Yemen	3,495	X	106	X

	INDUSTRIAL CO_2[2]	LAND USE CO_2[3]	METHANE[4]	CFCs[5]
EUROPE	4,347,794	X	26,000	180
Albania	9,732	X	95	X
Austria	51,699	X	310	3
Belgium	98,104	X	450	4
Bulgaria	106,969	X	330	1
Czechoslovakia[6]	226,347	X	820	4
Denmark	47,009	X	270	2
Finland	51,300	X	180	1
France	357,163	X	2,600	24
Germany	641,398	X	3,680	34
Greece	70,920	X	360	4
Hungary	64,076	X	410	3
Iceland	1,942	X	16	0
Ireland	29,352	X	430	2
Italy	389,747	X	2,000	25
Luxembourg	9,266	X	7	0
Malta	1,674	X	8	0
Netherlands	124,990	X	1,200	6
Norway	46,009	X	1,300	1
Poland	440,929	X	2,500	5
Portugal	40,912	X	350	4
Romania	212,193	X	1,500	2
Spain	203,227	X	1,600	17
Sweden	58,888	X	270	3
Switzerland	39,326	X	240	2
United Kingdom	568,451	X	3,900	25
U.S.S.R.[7]	3,804,001	X	34,000	67
Yugoslavia[8]	132,901	X	750	4
OCEANIA	291,248	12,000	6,200	9
Australia	257,480	X	5,000	8
Fiji	678	X	18	0
New Zealand	26,176	X	1,100	1
Papua New Guinea	2,250	12,000	15	X
Solomon Islands	161	X	1	X

[1]Greenhouse gases are those gases, occurring either naturally or through human activities, that enhance the ability of the Earth's atmosphere to trap and retain heat energy. Heat energy is solar energy that has been absorbed by the Earth's land and water surfaces, converted from light energy to long-wave or heat energy, and radiated back to warm the atmosphere. Many atmospheric scientists believe that an increase in the atmospheric content of greenhouse gases through fossil-fuel burning, forest clearance, and other anthropogenic processes may cause global warming.

[2]Industrial carbon dioxide results from the combustion of solid, liquid, and gas fuels, gas flaring during petroleum extraction, and cement manufacture.

[3]Land use carbon dioxide generation is produced by land use changes that create higher than normal emissions; chief among these is forest clearance by burning, but the category would also include wetlands restoration, irrigation agriculture, and livestock feeding.

[4]Methane (CH_4) is produced chiefly from oil and natural gas extraction and distribution, coal mining, wetland rice agriculture, municipal solid waste decomposition, and livestock.

[5]CFCs, or chlorofluorocarbons, are produced by a wide variety of industrial and domestic uses, including propellant sprays and refrigeration coolants.

[6]On January 1, 1993, Czechoslovakia was separated by peaceful agreement into two independent countries, the Czech Republic and the Slovak Republic. At the time of this printing, information was not yet available for these two separate countries.

[7]At the time of this printing, separate statistical data on the countries of the Commonwealth of Independent States were not yet available, nor were there available data on the former Soviet republics that are not members of the C.I.S. The data for the former U.S.S.R. thus include information for Russia and the other Commonwealth countries of Armenia, Azerbaijan, Belarus, Kazakhstan, Kyrgyzstan, Moldova, Tajikistan, Turkmenistan, Ukraine, and Uzbekistan, along with the non-Commonwealth countries of Estonia, Georgia, Latvia, and Lithuania.

[8]At the time of this printing, separate statistical data on the countries that made up the former state of Yugoslavia were not yet available. The data for Yugoslavia thus include information for the Federal Republic of Yugoslavia (Serbia and Montenegro) and the independent countries of Bosnia-Herzegovina, Croatia, Macedonia, and Slovenia.

Source: World Resources 1992–93.

Credits

Crabb, C. (1993, January). "Soiling the planet." *Discover, 1992, The Year in Science,* Vol. 14, no. 1, pp. 74-75.

DeBlij, H. J., & Muller, P. (1992). *Geography: Regions and concepts* (6th ed. revised). New York: John Wiley & Sons.

Domke, K. (1988). *War and the changing global system.* New Haven, CT: Yale University Press.

Johnson, D. (1977). *Population, society, and desertification.* New York: United Nations Conference on Desertification, United Nations Environment Programme.

Köppen, W., & Geiger, R. (1954). *Klima der erde* [Climate of the earth]. Darmstadt, Germany: Justus Perthes.

Lindeman, M. (1990). *The United States and the Soviet Union: Choices for the 21st century.* Guilford, CT: The Dushkin Publishing Group.

Murphy, R. E. (1968). "Landforms of the world." Map supplement no. 9, *Annals of the Association of American Geographers,* Vol. 58, No. 1, pp. 198-200.

National Oceanic and Atmospheric Administration (1990-92). Unpublished data. Washington, DC: NOAA.

Population Reference Bureau (1992). *1992 world population data sheet.* New York: Population Reference Bureau.

Rourke, J. T. (1993). *International politics on the world stage* (4th ed.). Guilford, CT: The Dushkin Publishing Group.

Spector, L. S., & Smith, J. R. (1990). *Nuclear ambitions: The spread of nuclear weapons.* Boulder, CO: Westview Press.

United Nations Population Fund. (1992). *The state of the world's population.* New York: United Nations Population Fund.

U.S. Arms Control and Disarmament Agency. (1991). *World military expenditures and arms transfers.* Washington, DC: USGPO.

The world almanac and book of facts (1992). New York: Pharos Books.

The World Bank. (1991). *World development report.* Geneva, Switzerland: The World Bank.

World Health Organization. (1990). *World health statistics annual.* Geneva, Switzerland: World Health Organization.

World Resources Institute. (1992). *World resources, 1992-1993.* New York: Oxford University Press.